GOOD HOUSEKEEPING
COMPLETE
microwave
COOKBOOK

EBURY PRESS
LONDON

At the time of going to press, it has been recommended by the
Ministry of Agriculture, Fisheries and Food that the use of cling
film should be avoided in microwave cooking. When a recipe
requires you to use cling film, you should either cover with a lid
or a plate, leaving a gap to let steam escape.

Published by Ebury Press
Division of the National Magazine Company Ltd.
Colquhoun House
27–37 Broadwick Street
London W1V 1FR

First impression 1984
Second impression 1985
Third impression 1985
Fourth impression 1985
Fifth impression 1986
Sixth impression 1986
Seventh impression 1987
Eighth impression 1988

ISBN 0 85223 362 0 (hardback)
ISBN 0 85223 367 1 (paperback)

Edited by Nancy Anthony
Designed by Roger Daniels
Illustrations by Hayward and Martin Studios

Colour photography by Paul Kemp

Jacket photograph shows, from top,
Minted Courgette Soup (page 38), Chinese-Style Chicken with
Vegetables (page 71) and Chilled Lemon Cream (page 102)

Filmset by Inforum Ltd
Printed and bound in Great Britain
by Butler and Tanner Ltd, Frome, Somerset

Contents

Foreword

This book has been written to help today's busy cook successfully prepare meals in minutes. The cooking techniques as presented here are straightforward and simple, with many clear illustrations, to help the cook master microwave cooking. By explaining how microwaves work and their affects on food, you will understand just how easy cooking food in a microwave oven really is.

Information about cooking and defrosting times for most foods is presented in easy to follow charts, and there is a complete guide to adapting your favourite recipes from a conventional oven to the microwave, making this book an invaluable reference source for all microwave cooking. All the recipes in this book can be cooked in any microwave oven.

We see the microwave oven as a complement to, rather than a complete replacement for the conventional oven. Over 150 simple and delicious recipes, many of which use both microwave and conventional cooking techniques, have been specially developed and tested. We tell you which foods and types of cooking are most suitable for the microwave and show you how to rethink menu planning and co-ordinate cooking so that you get the most from your microwave.

Introduction

Speed of cooking may be the most obvious reason for having a microwave oven. However, along with the great time savings – a jacket potato will be done in 4 minutes instead of one hour – the microwave reheats food so that it looks and tastes freshly cooked and can be used to defrost food in just a fraction of the time it normally takes. For these reasons, the microwave offers great flexibility and spontaneity with family meal planning and cooking.

● The microwave oven is simple to operate and requires no special installation. Where space is a problem the oven can be sited in rooms other than the kitchen since there are minimal cooking odours. The oven's interior is cool so there are no baked-on spillages to be scrubbed off. Cleaning basically entails wiping the interior with a damp cloth after each use. As many foods can be cooked and served in the same dish, washing up is kept to a minimum and there are no saucepans to scour and clean.

● The ovens are stringently tested in the manufacturer's laboratory to ensure that they are safe. Microwave ovens are the perfect cooking appliance for the elderly, blind and disabled. Even children can learn to operate them.

● Not only does the microwave use no more energy than the conventional hob ring, but energy is only used when food is being cooked. There is no fuel-wasting pre-heating or cooling down of the oven and the oven switches off automatically at a time preset by the cook. Because cooking times are generally much shorter in a microwave then in a conventional cooker, energy and money are saved.

● As any cook recognises, the time and fuel-saving advantages of a microwave are not in themselves sufficient reasons to invest in one. Food must also be well cooked and attractive to serve.

Indeed, some foods actually seem to improve in taste and texture when microwaved. The natural fresh flavours of fish and vegetables are enhanced and cakes rise higher than those cooked in the conventional way. Small tasks like melting chocolate and butter can be done with less risk of scorching.

Cooking is done in a minimum of liquid and for a short time only, so foods such as vegetables retain their colour and vital nutrients. Food can also be cooked with a minimum or no added fat.

The limitations of a microwave oven

All this said, the oven does have its limitations. Meat, pastry crusts and cakes do not brown and do not have crispy surfaces when cooked in a microwave. Certain foods such as Yorkshire puddings, roast potatoes and meringues cannot be cooked successfully in a microwave, nor can it be used for deep frying.

Although it is possible to leave food unattended in a microwave, it must be checked throughout cooking. For example, if a recipe says to cook a dish for 9 minutes, stirring twice – set the timer for 4½ minutes, stir the dish, then reset the timer for another 4½ minutes. New cooking techniques are necessary but once you understand how a microwave cooks food these new techniques become clear and, with a little practice, second nature. (See pages 14–15 for special cooking techniques.)

> ### WARNING
>
> Metal must not come into contact with the interior of the oven. Do not use metal containers and do not wrap or cover food with foil. If absolutely necessary, shield parts of food with a very small piece of foil to prevent overcooking. Make sure the foil is smooth and does not touch the sides of the microwave as it will damage the oven. Foil incorrectly used can cause sparks which will damage the oven and could be a fire hazard.

About your microwave oven

The microwave oven is an efficient and simple kitchen appliance. Its basic structure has very few moving parts and it is designed to ensure that microwaves stay inside the oven. There is a wide range of models available, from a small model with one or two power settings, to a large sophisticated microwave with a number of different settings.

Types and sizes

Since microwaves are connected to a normal 13- or 15-amp three-pin earthed plug, these ovens do not have to be sited in the kitchen but can be placed on a countertop or sturdy trolley. Built-in models are also available. A two-level microwave cooker has a rack or shelf in the oven giving two cooking positions: food on the shelf cooks more quickly than that on the base.

If you are thinking of replacing your conventional cooker, combination ovens are now available in which you can cook by both microwave and conventional methods in the same oven, combining the advantages of short cooking times in the microwave and the browning and crisping facilities of a conventional cooker. Full-size combination microwave and conventional cookers complete with hob are the latest addition to the world of hi-tech cooking.

Microwave ovens come in a variety of sizes. Which one you choose depends to a large extent on where the oven will be sited and the space available. However, no matter what position you choose, the microwave must be well ventilated. If vents, which allow moisture to escape during cooking, are at the top of the oven, it should not be sited under a cupboard or shelf. If these vents are at the back, the oven should not be positioned against a wall.

Power settings and controls

The simplest models have on/off switches, some have HIGH, MEDIUM, LOW or DEFROST dials, while more sophisticated ovens have up to 11 settings or controls which in some models are expressed in cooking methods such as 'roast', 'simmer' and 'reheat'. These variable power controls give greater flexibility when selecting the speed of cooking and take into account the fact that some foods require gentle cooking while others are best cooked quickly.

Special features

TURNTABLE AND STIRRERS To ensure even cooking, food must be turned and a turntable does this automatically.

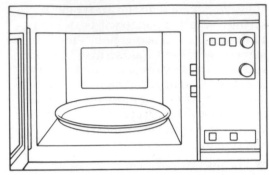

However, it is still necessary to reposition the food by hand. Some ovens are also equipped with automatic stirrers which are situated in the roof of the microwave. A stirrer helps to equally distribute microwaves throughout the oven.

TEMPERATURE PROBE OR FOOD SENSOR Using a temperature probe, food can be cooked by temperature rather than by a set time. This is inserted into the food during cooking and set to the desired temperature. When the correct temperature is reached the oven switches off or, as in some models, the oven automatically keeps the food warm until it is needed.

Although probes are very useful for cooking meat and poultry they can only be connected to one part of the food, and therefore can be unreliable. For this reason, conventional thermometers inserted after cooking or conventional techniques for testing to see if food is cooked, are usually more reliable than probes or food sensors.

MEMORY CONTROLS With a memory control it is possible to begin cooking on HIGH and then automatically switch to LOW partway through cooking time. Most oven memories allow you to programme two or three power settings, cooking for different times or to different temperatures. Some ovens can be programmed to keep food at a required temperature for a set length of time.

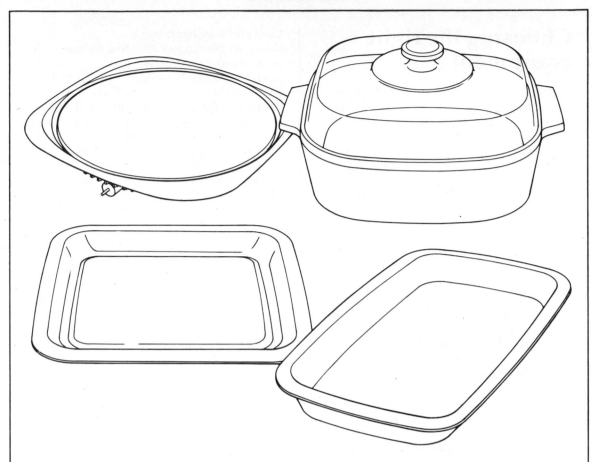

BROWNING ELEMENT OR GRILL This device works in the same way as a conventional grill and is especially useful for those for whom the microwave is their main or sole cooking appliance since there is no need to transfer a dish to a conventional grill for browning.

Extras

BROWNING DISH Because of the short cooking times, most foods do not have time to brown. A specially coated dish can be purchased which allows browning, searing, grilling or frying during cooking. The dish must be preheated – this takes up to 10 minutes – so that the coating on the dish absorbs enough microwave energy to produce a hot cooking surface. The surface is then greased and food is pressed on to the dish to brown it. A deep browning dish can first be used for browning before adding the other ingredients in the recipe to the dish.

Browning skillets, griddles and plates are other useful accessories for browning. Skillets and plates have a groove to allow fat to drain away during browning. These dishes can all be purchased separately.

MICROWAVE ROASTING RACK Specially designed for using in the microwave, a roasting rack is not only useful for elevating meat and poultry during cooking but bread and pastry can be placed on one to allow air to circulate underneath – this helps retain their crisp surfaces.

MICROWAVE THERMOMETER This is useful for cooking meat in ovens not equipped with a temperature probe and replaces a conventional meat thermometer which (because of its mercury content) cannot be used in a microwave oven. A conventional meat thermometer should only be used *after* food is cooked.

HOW TO TEST THAT CONTAINERS AND UTENSILS ARE 'MICROSAFE'
Place the dish in the oven along with a tumbler half-full of water. Microwave at full power for 1 minute. A dish is microwave safe if the water is warm and the dish is cool. The dish can be used for short periods if both the dish and water are warm but if the dish is hot and the water is still cold, the dish is unsuitable.

Choosing the right equipment

Containers for cooking in a microwave oven must be made from a moisture-free material which allows microwaves to pass through them with as little restriction as possible, like sunlight passing through a glass window. Metal reflects microwaves and *should not be used*. If metal dishes are used they can cause arcing (small sparks) and damage the microwave oven.

A wide variety of containers you probably have on hand can be used and a whole new range of specially designed ovenware is also available.

Although microwaves are not absorbed by the cooking dish, it may become hot during cooking because heat is conducted from the food to the container. This happens either during long periods of cooking or with foods containing a high proportion of sugar or fat, since microwaves are attracted to fat and sugar. For this reason, less durable containers such as those made of paper, should be reserved for brief cooking times such as warming, reheating or cooking vegetables.

Conventional containers

Ovenglass containers are ideal for use in the microwave. Not only are they interchangeable between conventional and microwave ovens, but there is the added advantage of watching food cook in the dish. Some types of *oven-to-tableware* can be used for freezing, for conventional cooking and grilling and microwave cooking as well. Use *china* (including dinner plates) for heating meals and ordinary *glass* for gentle warming.

Unglazed pottery and *earthenware* will absorb moisture and therefore absorb microwaves, thus slowing down cooking. However, this may be used to advantage: a chicken brick can be presoaked in water and used to slowly cook a casserole or stew in the microwave. For quick cooking, however, avoid using these containers.

Although prolonged use of either *wood* or *wicker* will cause them to crack, they are ideal for using to warm foods such as bread rolls.

Microwave ovenware

Cooking equipment designed specially for use in the microwave oven is usually made from materials through which microwaves

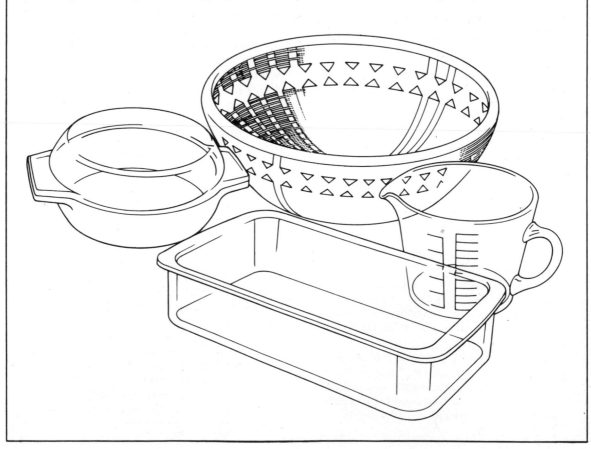

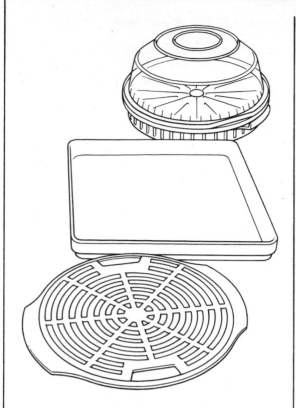

Covering

Dishes are covered during microwaving to help retain moisture in the food and to speed up the cooking process. Generally, foods which do not need to be stirred during cooking are covered tightly with cling film and foods which need stirring are three-quarters covered so that you can put a spoon in the dish to use for stirring without removing the film. Foods which need to be dry on the surface such as cakes and roasts are not normally covered.

Special microwave dishes with lids are available, otherwise ordinary *cling film* is very useful as a tight-fitting cover, though microwave cling film is slightly tougher than ordinary cling film and will adhere to plastic as well as glass. For long periods of cooking, cling film should be turned back at one corner. Take care when removing cling film from cooked dishes, as the steam will scald your hands. Starting on the side furthest away, pull back the cling film towards you. Ordinary non-metal casserole lids and even upturned plates can be used to cover food.

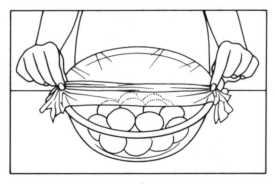

pass more quickly than they do through conventionally used materials like china and glass. Always check manufacturer's instructions to see if the ovenware can withstand freezer and/or conventional oven temperatures as well as the microwave. Many ranges come with a set of two lids – one for storing or freezing and one for cooking in the microwave. Microwave ovenware offers a complete range of containers from casseroles to loaf dishes, patty 'tins', 'roasting' racks, baking sheets and even a popcorn popper.

Container shape and size

The more regular the shape of your container the more even the cooking will be. Important for efficient microwave cooking are; well-rounded corners, straight sides and concave undersides for even food distribution. A round dish, particularly a ring-shaped container, will allow cooking to be more even than an oval dish as overcooking or drying out can occur at the 'ends' of these dishes.

Choose cooking dishes large enough to hold the quantity of food and avoid over-filling which can cause spillages and prevent even cooking. Dishes should be large enough to hold foods such as fish, chicken joints or chops in a single layer.

Do not use tight-fitting plastic lids or balance the lids on top of the container as they might well be sucked into the food during microwaving. *Boil-in-the-bags*, *roasting bags* and *polythene bags* should always be tied loosely with an elastic band or string and not with a metal tag. The bags should be slit before microwaving to prevent them bursting.

Use *greaseproof paper* as a loose-fitting cover for foods which may splatter during cooking, such as bacon. *Absorbent kitchen paper* can be used for breads, pastry and baked potatoes (for warming and cooking) to absorb moisture and is a useful cover when cooking bacon as it absorbs the fat and makes it crisper. Always quickly remove paper after microwaving, otherwise it may stick to the food.

How microwaves cook food

From the earliest days of cooking over an open fire to today's sophisticated fan-assisted ovens, cooking has consisted of applying heat to raw food in order to transform it into an appetising dish. The microwave oven is a revolutionary cooking appliance because heat is not applied to food. The microwaves in themselves contain no heat – instead heat is created in the food by the action of microwaves. Certain steps to mastering microwave cooking such as positioning dishes, rotating food, shielding and stirring make sense if you understand the basics.

What are microwaves?

Microwave energy is a type of electrical energy which is transmitted through space. Microwaves are electro-magnetic waves which fall into the same spectrum as the waves used in transmitting a television picture, radio sound, radar systems and sunlight. They are of a very short length which is why they are called *micro*waves.

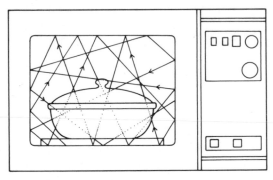

In a microwave oven electrical energy is converted to microwaves by a tube called a magnetron, which is similar to a television tube. The magnetron can only produce microwaves when both the oven door is shut and the timer is on. Microwaves enter the cavity of the oven and are distributed throughout the oven; in some ovens a fan called a 'stirrer' helps to distribute microwaves evenly. Microwaves are reflected by metal and because all microwave ovens have metal walls (even though many are lined with acrylic), the oven cavity traps the microwaves and they bounce off all the walls, including the base and the glass door which has a metal mesh

screen through which the microwaves cannot pass.

Microwaves pass through non-metal substances such as plastic, paper, wood, glass and ceramics. But their most important characteristic is that they are absorbed by the food they come into contact with – in fact, microwaves will be absorbed by anything containing water and this includes all food.

How food is cooked

Microwaves only penetrate food to a depth of 5 cm (2 inches). Yet, microwaved food can be cooked through to the centre. The agitation of water molecules on the surface of food is just like rubbing your hands together to make them warm. It produces heat and spreads through the food by conduction. Thus, food more than 5 cm (2 inches) thick cooks by a combination of microwave action and heat conduction. When microwave energy is switched off, food will continue to cook due to heat conduction; this is why many recipes call for a period of 'standing time' after the food has been taken out of the oven.

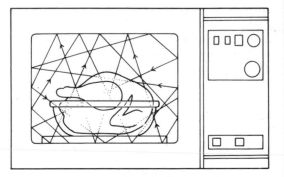

Factors which affect the way food cooks

FOOD QUALITY Cooking rarely disguises poor quality food and the microwave oven is no exception. In fact, because natural flavours of vegetables and fish seem more pronounced when cooked in the microwave, these foods must be very fresh. Similarly, herbs and spices retain their distinctive flavours when used as part of a microwaved dish – staleness cannot be disguised.

FOOD TEMPERATURE Just as cold food takes longer to reheat or cook than food at room temperature when cooking conventionally, it will also take longer when microwaving. However, because 1 minute can make the difference between success and failure in a microwave oven, food temperature is crucial when calculating cooking times.

FOOD COMPOSITION Since microwaves are attracted to the water molecules in food, moist foods tend to cook very well in the microwave. However, delicate foods like scallops, mushrooms and oysters, which are high in water content, should be cooked gently and stirred frequently to prevent them overcooking and toughening. Food microwaved for a relatively long time such as a whole turkey or a large chicken, will have time to brown.

Foods enclosed in a skin such as pulses may burst during cooking due to a build-up of pressure under the skin. For this reason eggs for 'frying', tomatoes, jacket potatoes and sausages are all pricked before microwaving. Eggs cannot be boiled in the microwave because the pressure which builds up under the shell may cause explosions; baked beans tend to pop during microwaving and are best microwaved on LOW.

Microwaves are also attracted to the sugar and fat molecules in foods, so foods high in these substances will heat very rapidly. Concentrations of fat or sugar such as the fat in a piece of meat or the fruit filling in a pie will become very hot before the rest of the food does. After microwaving, during 'standing time', the heat becomes equalised in the food.

Foods high in salt tend to dry out or toughen in a microwave, so baste with unsalted butter for best results and do not salt vegetables before cooking them.

FOOD QUANTITY The more food microwaved at one time, the longer the cooking takes because microwave energy has to disperse over a greater surface area of food. One jacket potato will take about 4 minutes to cook on HIGH, whereas two potatoes will take about 6–8 minutes. If doubling the quantity of food called for in a recipe, increase microwaving cooking times by between one-third and one-half. If quantities are reduced by half the cooking times can be reduced by a little more than half the stated time. Remember never to overload a microwave oven.

FOOD DENSITY OR TEXTURE The denser the food the longer it takes to cook because it takes longer for heat to be conducted to the centre of the food. Thick-textured meats take longer than breads and puddings. Similarly, minced meat will cook in less time than a steak.

FOOD SIZE AND SHAPE Small pieces of the same type of food cook more quickly in a microwave than larger pieces: a whole joint naturally takes longer to cook than small cubes of meat. To ensure even cooking, food should always be cut to the same size and shape.

Microwaves will naturally penetrate thin pieces of food quicker than thick pieces. Meat which is uneven in shape, such as a leg of lamb, will cook unevenly unless it is tied or moulded into an even shape.

UNDERSTANDING POWER SETTINGS AND HEAT CONTROLS

When manufacturers refer to a 700-watt oven they are referring to the oven's *power output*; its *input*, which is indicated on the back of the oven, would be double that figure.

The higher the wattage of an oven the faster the rate of cooking, thus food cooked at 700 watts on full power will cook in half the time as food cooked at 350 watts. That said, the actual cooking performance of one 700-watt oven may vary from another with the same wattage because factors like oven cavity size affect cooking performance.

Unlike conventional ovens the various microwave ovens have yet to be standardised. A HIGH or full power setting on one oven may be 500 watts while on another model HIGH or full power is 700 watts. The vast majority of ovens sold today are either 600-, 650- or 700-watt ovens but there are many ovens still in use which have between 400 and 500 watts.

In this book HIGH refers to full power output of 600–700 watts, MEDIUM corresponds to 60 per cent of full power and LOW is 35 per cent of full power. If your oven power output is lower than 600 watts, then you must allow a longer cooking and defrosting time for all recipes and charts in this book.

Special microwave cooking techniques

Special cooking techniques are used to ensure that food cooks evenly in the microwave, even the most advanced ovens cannot guarantee that food cooks evenly because of the very nature of microwave energy and the density of the food.

By following the simple master techniques of microwave cooking, food can be evenly cooked:

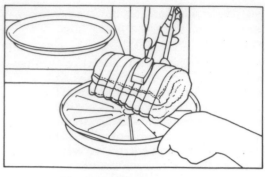

TURNING: Start cooking meat fat side down and turn it over during cooking.

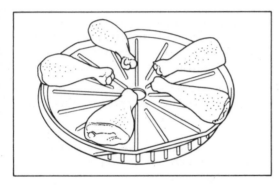

POSITIONING: Place thinner parts of food towards the centre of the dish. If possible arrange food such as fish fillets or chicken drumsticks in a circle, leaving the centre of the dish empty.

ROTATING: All ovens have a 'blind spot', even ovens with a turntable or stirrer. Food should be given a quarter turn three times during cooking. This is especially the case with large items of food – such as flans, cakes, pâtés or big pieces of meat – which cannot be stirred.

REPOSITIONING: Foods which are cooking more quickly on the outside of the dish are moved to the middle.

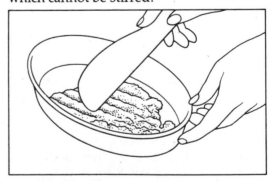

STIRRING: Food cut into pieces as in meat or fish casseroles or for sauces and stews and other 'liquid' dishes should be stirred instead of rotated, starting from the outside, bringing the food which is more cooked towards the centre.

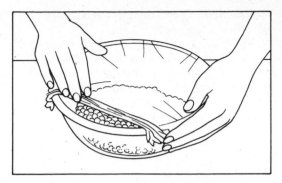

COVERING: Cover foods tightly with cling film when a moist, even heat is required such as with vegetables. Fold back a corner to allow some steam to escape and to make a gap for stirring.

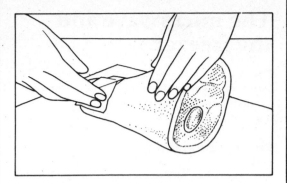

SHIELDING: Use small pieces of smooth foil to shield parts of food such as the protruding bones of a joint which tend to cook before the rest of the food. Make sure the foil does not touch the sides of the oven or it will damage the magnetron. Shield food only when necessary.

LINING: Cake containers other than plastic should be lined with greaseproof paper or cling film. Remove the paper or film as soon as the cake has been turned out to prevent sticking.

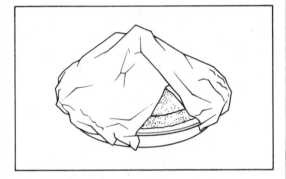

STANDING Remove food from the oven and, if it was not covered during cooking, cover it loosely with foil and leave to stand for the specified time. Keep an eye on quickly cooked foods (such as fish) as they can easily overcook during standing time.

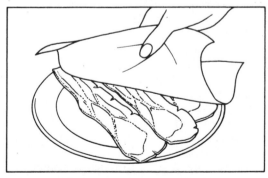

CRISPING: Loosely cover food like bacon with greaseproof paper or absorbent kitchen paper to absorb the fat and make it crisper.

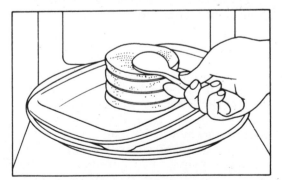

BROWNING: It is not possible to brown foods in the conventional way in a microwave oven. Instead, food can be browned using a special browning dish or it can be flashed under the grill.

The microwave and the freezer

The microwave oven helps make the freezer a more integral and accessible part of meal planning and is especially useful for impromptu meals.

Packing and sealing
When freezing food, bear in mind just how you eventually intend to use it. If you live alone or your family has an erratic meal-time schedule, cook food in batches and pack it in individual portions. With a microwave it is very easy for anyone – even non-cooks – to reheat single portions.

Pack food in containers suitable for using in both freezer and microwave; many containers can also withstand conventional oven temperatures as well. *Freezer to microwave ovenware* is designed especially for freezing conventionally cooked foods to be reheated in a microwave. *Paper board* is intended for using once and is ideal for pies, flans and other non-liquid dishes which require only a short-period microwaving.

Food frozen in deep foil containers should never be defrosted in the microwave. However, foil trays less than 2 cm (¾ inch) deep can be used because they are shallow enough to allow the microwaves to heat the food from the top – however, the tray must not touch the sides of the oven.

Boil-in-the-bags and *roasting bags* which are excellent for freezing stews, casseroles, vegetables and small joints can be put directly into the microwave.

Defrosting
In order for food to evenly and completely defrost it must be microwaved on LOW or the DEFROST setting, otherwise the surface of the food may dry out or even start to cook before the centre is thawed. Times for defrosting are usually based on an approximate power output of 30–35 per cent of 600–700 power output ovens. Some ovens defrost food by automatically switching on and off at a high setting to allow rest periods in between short bursts of microwaving. If your oven has no low control it is possible to defrost manually by turning off the oven every 30 seconds and allowing food to stand for 1½ minutes

before turning the oven on again for another 30 seconds.

Most foods are defrosted by being put in the microwave for a set time and then left to stand to complete the process. For this reason many foods will still be full of ice crystals in the centre but during standing will thaw out completely.

Use the same techniques for defrosting as you use for cooking food in the microwave: stir food when possible, moving still frozen parts to the outside of the dish; separate chunks of food to help speed defrosting; loosen up outer wrappings or packages and turn large items over several times; rotate the dish and reposition foods.

DRYING HERBS

If you have an abundance of fresh herbs, they can be preserved by drying them in the microwave. Not only do they retain their fresh flavours but they retain their natural colours. Herbs should be dried on a piece of absorbent kitchen paper and need to be stirred frequently – use your fingers – during microwaving so that they dry evenly and also do not become too brittle. Stir every 20 seconds during the first minute then every 5–10 seconds until dried. Microwave 50 g (2 oz) finely chopped parsley on HIGH for 5 minutes. Trim rosemary and basil leaves from their stalks and microwave 25 g (1 oz) leaves for 2–2½ minutes on HIGH. After drying they can be chopped or crushed with your fingers. Store dried herbs in screw-top jars in a cool dark place.

Crab filled courgette slices (Starter) *opposite*

DEFROSTING MEAT

Frozen meat exudes a lot of liquid during defrosting and because microwaves are attracted to water, the liquid should be poured off or mopped up with absorbent kitchen paper when it collects, otherwise defrosting will take longer. Start defrosting a joint in its wrapper and remove as soon as possible – usually after one-quarter of the defrosting time. Place the joint on a microwave roasting rack so that it does not stand in liquid during defrosting.

Remember to turn over a large piece of meat. If the joint shows signs of cooking give the meat a 'rest' period of 20 minutes. Alternatively, shield the 'thin ends' or parts which will thaw more quickly, with small, smooth pieces of foil. A joint is thawed when a skewer can easily pass through the thickest part of the meat. Chops and steaks should be repositioned during defrosting; test them by pressing the surface with your fingers – the meat should feel cold to the touch and give in the thickest part.

Do not allow foil used for shielding to touch the sides of the oven.

Type	Appoximate time on LOW setting	Special instructions
BEEF		
Boned roasting joints (sirloin, topside)	8–10 minutes per 450 g (1 lb)	*Turn* over regularly during defrosting and rest if the meat shows signs of cooking. *Stand* for 1 hour.
Joints on bone (rib of beef)	10–12 minutes per 450 g (1 lb)	*Shield* bone end with small, smooth pieces of foil and overwrap it with cling film. *Turn* joint over during defrosting. The meat will still be icy in the centre but will complete thawing if you leave it to stand for 1 hour.
Minced beef	8–10 minutes per 450 g (1 lb)	*Stand* for 10 minutes.
Cubed steak	6–8 minutes per 450 g (1 lb)	*Stand* for 10 minutes.
Steak (sirloin, rump)	8–10 minutes per 450 g (1 lb)	*Stand* for 10 minutes.
Beefburgers standard (50 g/2 oz)	2 burgers: 2 minutes 4 burgers: 2–3 minutes	Can be cooked from frozen, without defrosting, if preferred.
quarter-pounder	2 burgers: 2–3 minutes 4 burgers: 5 minutes	
burger buns	2 buns: 2 minutes	*Stand* burger buns for 2 minutes.
LAMB/VEAL		
Boned rolled joint (loin, leg, shoulder)	5–6 minutes per 450 g (1 lb)	As for boned roasting joints of beef above. *Stand* for 30–45 minutes.
On the bone (leg and shoulder)	5–6 minutes per 450 g (1 lb)	As for beef joints on bone above. *Stand* for 30–45 minutes.
Minced lamb or veal	8–10 minutes per 450 g (1 lb)	*Stand* for 10 minutes.
Chops	8–10 minutes per 450 g (1 lb)	*Separate* during defrosting. *Stand* for 10 minutes.
PORK		
Boned rolled joint (loin, leg)	7–8 minutes per 450 g (1 lb)	As for boned roasting joints of beef above. *Stand* for 1 hour.

Pizza flan (Eggs and Cheese) *opposite*

Type	Approximate time on LOW setting	Special instructions
On the bone (leg, hand)	7–8 minutes per 450 g (1 lb)	As for beef joints on bone above. *Stand* for 1 hour.
Tenderloin	8–10 minutes per 450 g (1 lb)	*Stand* for 10 minutes.
Chops	8–10 minutes per 450 g (1 lb)	*Separate* during defrosting and arrange 'spoke' fashion. *Stand* for 10 minutes.
Sausages	5–6 minutes per 450 g (1 lb)	*Separate* during defrosting. *Stand* for 5 minutes.
OFFAL		
Liver	8–10 minutes per 450 g (1 lb)	*Separate* during defrosting. *Stand* for 5 minutes.
Kidney	6–9 minutes per 450 g (1 lb)	*Separate* during defrosting. *Stand* for 5 minutes.
BACON		
Rashers	2 minutes per 225 g (8 oz) packet	*Remove* slices from pack and separate after defrosting. *Stand* for 6–8 minutes.

VEGETABLES

Prepare vegetables for the freezer by using the microwave. Instead of immersing vegetables in large pans of boiling water when they will start to lose some of their colour and nutrients, 'blanch' them in the microwave in only 45–60 ml (4–5 tbsp) unsalted boiling water. Microwave vegetables on HIGH for 3–4 minutes, stirring once, until the vegetables are heated through. Refresh under cold water, drain and pack.

Frozen vegetables can be cooked in the microwave straight from the freezer and if packed in heavy-duty polythene bags, boil-in-the-bags or other non-metal container, the vegetables can go directly into the microwave. First pierce the bag and place the bag on a plate. Make sure to add any water to the bag or container, if necessary. Vegetables with a high water content such as spinach and mushrooms do not need added water.

DEFROSTING POULTRY AND GAME

Poultry or game should be thawed in its freezer wrapping which should be pierced first and the metal tag removed. During defrosting, pour off liquid that collects in the bag. Finish defrosting in a bowl of cold water with the bird still in its bag. Chicken portions can be thawed in the polystyrene trays.

Type	Approximate time on LOW setting	Special instructions
Whole chicken or duckling	6–8 minutes per 450 g (1 lb)	Remove giblets. *Stand* in cold water for 30 minutes.
Whole turkey	10–12 minutes per 450 g (1 lb)	Remove giblets. *Stand* in cold water for 2–3 hours.
Chicken portions	5–7 minutes per 450 g (1 lb)	*Separate* during defrosting. *Stand* for 10 minutes.
Poussin, grouse, pheasant, pigeon, quail	5–7 minutes per 450 g (1 lb)	

DEFROSTING FISH AND SHELLFISH

Separate fish cutlets, fillets or steaks as soon as possible during defrosting. Like poultry, it is best to finish defrosting whole fish in cold water to prevent drying out of the surface. Arrange scallops and prawns in a circle and cover with absorbent kitchen paper to help absorb liquid; remove pieces from the oven as soon as defrosted.

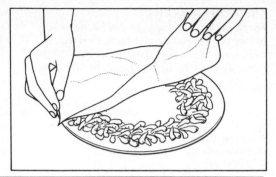

Type	Approximate time on LOW setting	Special instructions
White fish fillets or cutlets, eg cod, coley, haddock, halibut, or whole plaice or sole	3–4 minutes per 450 g (1 lb) plus 2–3 minutes	*Stand* for 5 minutes after each 2–3 minutes.
Oily fish, eg whole and gutted mackerel, herring, trout	2–3 minutes per 225 g (8 oz) plus 3–4 minutes	*Stand* for 5 minutes between defrosts and for 5 minutes afterwards.
Kipper fillets	2–3 minutes per 225 g (8 oz)	As for oily fish above.
Lobster tails, crab claws, etc	3–4 minutes per 225 g (8 oz) plus 2–3 minutes	As for oily fish above.
Crabmeat	2–3 minutes per 450 g (1 lb) block plus 2–3 minutes	As for oily fish above.
Prawns, shrimps, scampi	2½ minutes per 100 g (4 oz) 3–4 minutes per 225 g (8 oz)	*Pierce* plastic bag if necessary. *Stand* for 2 minutes. *Separate* with a fork after 2 minutes. *Stand* for minutes, then plunge into cold water and drain.

DEFROSTING DESSERTS

Type	Approximate time on LOW setting	Special instructions
Cheesecake with fruit topping	about 3–4 minutes for 23 cm (9 in) diameter cheesecake	*Place* on serving dish. *Stand* for 20 minutes.
Fruit pie	4–5 minutes for 650 g (26 oz) pie	*Stand* for 5–10 minutes. *Do not* make on metal tin.
Mousse	30 seconds per individual mousse	*Remove* lid before defrosting. *Stand* for 15–20 minutes.
Trifle	45–60 seconds per individual trifle	*Remove* lid before defrosting. *Stand* for 15–20 minutes.

DEFROSTING FRUIT

For those fruits which should be defrosted before cooking and even for frozen fruits defrosted to eat raw, use the microwave to partially thaw fruits and finish by standing.

Type	Quantity	Approximate time on LOW setting	Special instructions
Soft fruit, eg strawberries, raspberries	225 g (8 oz) 450 g (1 lb)	3–5 minutes 6–8 minutes	*Stir* gently during defrosting. *Stand* until completely defrosted, stirring occasionally.
Fruit juice concentrate	178 ml (6¼ oz) can	2–3 minutes	*Remove* the collar and lid. *Stand* for 3–5 minutes.

DEFROSTING BAKED GOODS AND PASTRY DOUGH

To absorb the moisture of thawing cakes, breads and pastry place them on absorbent kitchen paper (remove as soon as defrosted to prevent sticking). For greater crispness, place baked goods and the paper on a microwave rack or elevate food on an upturned bowl to allow the air to circulate underneath.

Type	Quantity	Approximate time on LOW setting	Special instructions
BREAD			
Loaf, whole Loaf, whole	1 large 1 small	6–8 minutes 4–6 minutes	*Uncover* and place on absorbent kitchen paper. *Turn* over during defrosting. *Stand* for 5–15 minutes.
Loaf, sliced Loaf, sliced	1 large 1 small	6–8 minutes 4–6 minutes	*Defrost* in original wrapper but remove any metal tags. *Stand* for 10–15 minutes.
Slice of bread	25 g (1 oz)	10–15 seconds	*Place* on absorbent kitchen paper. *Time* carefully. *Stand* for 1–2 minutes.
Bread rolls, tea cakes, scones, etc.	2 4	15–20 seconds 25–35 seconds	*Place* on absorbent kitchen paper. *Time* carefully. *Stand* for 2–3 minutes.
Crumpets	2	15–20 seconds	As for bread rolls above.
CAKES AND PASTRIES			
Cakes	2 small 4 small	30–60 seconds 1–1½ minutes	*Place* on absorbent kitchen paper. *Stand* for 5 minutes.
Sponge cake	450 g (1 lb)	1–1½ minutes	*Place* on absorbent kitchen paper. *Test* and turn after 1 minute. *Stand* for 5 minutes.

Type	Quantity	Approximate time on LOW setting	Special instructions
Jam doughnuts	2 4	45–60 seconds 45–90 seconds	*Place* on absorbent kitchen paper. *Stand* for 5 minutes.
Cream doughnuts	2 4	45–60 seconds 1¼–1¾ minutes	*Place* on absorbent kitchen paper. *Check* after half the defrosting time. *Stand* for 10 minutes.
Cream éclairs	2 4	45 seconds 1–1½ minutes	*Stand* for 5–10 minutes. *Stand* for 15–20 minutes.
Choux buns	4 small	1–1½ minutes	*Stand* for 20–30 minutes.
PASTRY			
Shortcrust and puff	227 g (8 oz) packet 397 g (14oz) packet	1 minute 2 minutes	*Stand* for 20 minutes. *Stand* for 20–30 minutes.

DEFROSTING DAIRY PRODUCTS

Type	Approximate time on LOW setting	Special instructions
Butter or margarine	1½–2 minutes per 250 g (9 oz) packet	*Remove* wrapping and place block on absorbent kitchen paper. *Stand* for 5 minutes.
Cream, whipped	1–2 minutes per 300 ml (½ pint)	*Remove* metal lid if necessary. *Stand* for 10–15 minutes.
Cream cheese	1–1½ minutes per 75 g (3 oz)	*Remove* foil wrapping. *Place* on absorbent kitchen paper. *Stand* for 10–15 minutes.

DEFROSTING SAUCES AND SOUPS

Type	Approximate time on HIGH setting	Special instructions
White sauce	5 minutes per 300 ml (½ pint)	*Pour* into a large bowl and beat until smooth.
Soups	5 minutes per 300 ml (½ pint) 8 minutes per 900 ml (1½ pints)	*Shake* and *stir* frequently during defrosting. *Add* cream or yogurt after defrosting.

Cooking food in the microwave oven

MEAT

Meat will shrink less and retain more juices when microwaved. Remember that because meat does not brown on the outside when cooked in the microwave it will not look cooked, which is why it is important to follow cooking times and to allow the meat to stand, tented in foil, to finish cooking.

Even-sized compact shapes cook more evenly in a microwave, making boned rolled joints ideal. For the best results, mould and tie meat into an even shape for cooking. Select meat which is marbled with fat rather than meat with large sections of fat because microwaves are attracted to fat and large sections of fat will

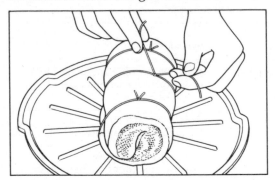

prevent the meat from cooking evenly. Small bony ends of joints can be shielded with very small pieces of smooth foil overwrapped with cling film. This prevents the thinner parts of a joint from overcooking.

Avoid seasoning meat with salt as it can toughen the surface during cooking – the exception is the rind of a joint of pork which can be rubbed with salt to make a crisp crackling. Start roasting meat fatty side down and turn it over halfway through cooking time. To help meat to brown, baste it with unsalted butter during cooking; elevating the joint high in the oven also helps browning as does using roasting bags or glass-covered casseroles. Bacon joints can be cooked quickly in the microwave, then glazed and quickly browned and crisped for a short time under the grill or in a hot oven. Smoked bacon joints have a higher salt content than green bacon and tend to dehydrate slightly when microwaved.

When preparing bacon rashers and chops remember to remove rinds and snip around the fatty edge of a chop to prevent it from curling. These foods, as well as steaks, can be microwaved on a browning dish or skillet. If a crisp, brown outside is desired, sausages, chops and steaks can be cooked in the microwave and then flashed under the grill.

Type	Time/Setting	Microwave Cooking Technique(s)
BEEF		
Boned roasting joint (sirloin, topside)	per 450 g (1 lb) Rare: 5–6 minutes on HIGH Medium: 7–8 minutes on HIGH Well: 8–10 minutes on HIGH	*Turn* joint over halfway through cooking time. *Stand* for 15–20 minutes tented with foil.
On the bone roasting joint (fore rib, back rib)	per 450 g (1 lb) Rare: 5 minutes on HIGH Medium: 6 minutes on HIGH Well: 8 minutes on HIGH	*Shield* bone end with small piece of foil during first half cooking time. *Turn* joint over halfway through cooking time. *Stand* as for boned joint.
LAMB/VEAL		
Boned rolled joint (loin, leg, shoulder)	per 450 g (1 lb) Medium: 7–8 minutes on HIGH Well: 8–10 minutes on HIGH	*Turn* joint over halfway through cooking time. *Stand* as for beef.
On the bone (leg and shoulder)	per 450 g (1 lb) Medium: 6–7 minutes on HIGH Well: 8–9 minutes on HIGH	*Shield* as for beef. *Position* fatty side down and turn over halfway through cooking time. *Stand* as for beef.

Type	Time/Setting	Microwave Cooking Technique(s)
Crown roast of lamb	9–10 minutes on MEDIUM per 450 g (1 lb) stuffed weight	*Shield* bone tips with foil and overwrap with cling film. *Reposition* partway through cooking time. *Stand* for 20 minutes with foil tenting.
Chops	1½ minutes on HIGH, then 1½–2 minutes on MEDIUM	*Cook* in preheated browning dish, or finish off under grill. *Position* with bone ends towards centre.

PORK

Type	Time/Setting	Microwave Cooking Technique(s)
Boned rolled joint (loin, leg)	8–10 minutes on HIGH per 450 g (1 lb)	As for boned rolled lamb above.
On the bone (leg, hand)	8–9 minutes on HIGH per 450 g (1 lb)	As for lamb on the bone above.
Chops	1 chop: 4–4½ minutes on HIGH 2 chops: 5–5½ minutes on HIGH 3 chops: 6–7 minutes on HIGH 4 chops: 6½–8 minutes on HIGH	*Cook* in preheated browning dish, or finish off under grill. *Position* with bone ends towards centre. *Cover* kidney, if attached, with greaseproof paper. *Stand* for 2 minutes for 1 chop, 3–5 minutes for 2–4 chops.

SAUSAGES

Type	Time/Setting	Microwave Cooking Technique(s)
SAUSAGES	2 sausages: 2½ minutes on HIGH 4 sausages: 4 minutes on HIGH	*Pierce* skins. *Cook* in preheated browning dish or finish off under grill. *Turn* occasionally during cooking.

BACON

Type	Time/Setting	Microwave Cooking Technique(s)
Joints	12–14 minutes on HIGH per 450 g (1 lb)	*Cook* in pierced roasting bag. *Turn* joint over partway through cooking time. *Stand* for 10 minutes, tented in foil.
Rashers	2 rashers: 2–2½ minutes on HIGH 4 rashers: 4–4½ minutes on HIGH 6 rashers: 5–6 minutes on HIGH 12 minutes on HIGH per 450 g (1 lb)	*Arrange* in a single layer. *Cover* with greaseproof paper to prevent splattering. *Cook* in preheated browning dish if liked. *Remove* paper immediately after cooking to prevent sticking. For large quantities: *Overlap* slices and place on microwave rack. *Reposition* three times during cooking.

OFFAL

Type	Time/Setting	Microwave Cooking Technique(s)
Liver (lamb and calves)	6–8 minutes on HIGH per 450 g (1 lb)	*Cover* with greaseproof paper to prevent splattering.
Kidneys	8 minutes on HIGH per 450 g (1 lb)	*Arrange* in a circle. *Cover* to prevent splattering. *Reposition* during cooking.
Tongue	20 minutes on HIGH per 450 g (1 lb)	*Reposition* during cooking.

POULTRY

Make sure frozen poultry is completely defrosted before microwaving.

Large chickens and turkeys will brown if cooked in roasting bags, especially if basted with unsalted butter. A little soy sauce, paprika or turmeric added to the basting liquid also helps give it a rich, browned appearance. A pierced roasting bag or glass-covered casserole will help small birds to brown or they can be browned in a browning dish or finished under a conventional grill. Poultry portions can be prepared in the same way, however small portions will not brown because of the short length of time required to cook them – they can of course be flashed under the grill when cooking is complete, or if the recipe includes a baste such as soy sauce, grilling will be unnecessary.

Poultry is cooked when a knife is inserted into the thickest part of the meat and the juices run clear.

Place ducks on a microwave roasting rack and spoon off the fat during cooking; crisp the skin quickly under a grill.

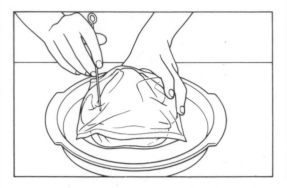

Type	Time/Setting	Microwave Cooking Technique(s)
CHICKEN		
Whole chicken	8–10 minutes on HIGH per 450 g (1 lb)	*Cook* in a roasting bag, breast side down and turn halfway through cooking. *Brown* under conventional grill, if preferred. *Stand* for 10–15 minutes.
Whole poussin	5 minutes on HIGH	*Cook* in a pierced roasting bag. *Turn* over as for whole chicken.
Portions	6–8 minutes on HIGH per 450 g (1 lb)	*Position* skin side up with thinner parts towards centre. *Reposition* halfway through cooking time. *Stand* for 5–10 minutes.
Boneless breast	2–3 minutes on HIGH	*Brown* under grill, if preferred.
DUCK		
Whole	7–10 minutes on HIGH per 450 g (1 lb)	*Turn* over as for whole chicken. *Stand* for 10–15 minutes.
Portions	4 x 300 g (11 oz) pieces: 10 minutes on HIGH, then 30–35 minutes on MEDIUM	*Position* and *reposition* as for chicken portions above.
TURKEY		
Whole	9–11 minutes on HIGH per 450 g (1 lb)	*Turn* over 3–4 times, depending on size, during cooking; start cooking breast side down. *Stand* for 10–15 minutes.
Boneless roll	10 minutes on HIGH per 450 g (1 lb)	*Turn* over halfway through cooking time.

FISH

Fish cooks superbly in a microwave, retaining its natural flavour and juices particularly well. But it must be monitored closely during microwaving as it can quickly overcook, especially delicate shellfish like scallops and oysters. To prevent fish from drying, brush with unsalted butter and microwave with the fish covered.

The skin of whole fish should be slashed to prevent it from bursting during microwaving. Arrange small whole fish in a cartwheel, tails towards the centre. The tail end of large fish may have to be shielded with a small piece of foil to

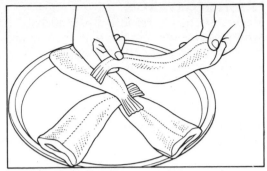

prevent the tail from burning or the flesh from drying out. Cook frozen cutlets and fillets in their original wrappings, which should be first slashed.

Type	Time/Setting	Microwave Cooking Technique(s)
Whole round fish (whiting, mullet, trout, carp, bream, small haddock)	3 minutes on HIGH per 450 g (1 lb)	*Slash* skin to prevent bursting. *Turn* over fish partway through cooking time. *Shield* tail with small pieces of smooth foil. *Reposition* fish if cooking more than 2.
Whole flat fish (plaice, sole)	3 minutes on HIGH	*Slash* skin. *Turn* dish partway through cooking time. *Shield* tail as for round fish.
Cutlets, steaks, fillets	4 minutes on HIGH per 450 g (1 lb)	*Position* thicker parts towards outside overlapping thin ends and separating with cling film. *Turn* over fillets and quarter-turn dish 3 times during cooking.
Smoked fish	4 minutes on HIGH per 450 g (1 lb)	Follow techniques for type of fish above.

RICE AND PASTA

Although there are no real time savings to cooking rice and pasta in the microwave it may be a more foolproof way of cooking as there is no risk of it sticking to the pan. Standing is necessary to complete cooking.

Dried peas and beans are not recommended for microwaving. The skins remain tough and will burst during cooking. Split lentils however can be successfully microwaved because they are not completely encased in a skin.

Type and quantity	Time on HIGH	Microwave cooking technique(s)
White long grain rice 225 g (8 oz)	10–12 minutes	*Stir* once during cooking. *Stand* for 10 minutes.
Brown rice, 100 g (4 oz)	30 minutes	As for white long grain.
Pasta shapes, 225 g (8 oz) dried	7 minutes	*Stir* once during cooking. *Stand* for 5 minutes.
Spaghetti, tagliatelli, 225 g (8 oz) dried	7–8 minutes	*Stand* for 10 minutes.

FRESH VEGETABLES

Vegetables need very little water added when microwaved. In this way they retain their colour, flavour and nutrients more than they would when cooked conventionally. They can be cooked in boil-in-the-bags, plastic containers and polythene bags – make sure there is a space for steam to escape.

Prepare vegetables for cooking in the same way as you would if conventionally cooking them. It is most important that food is cut to an even size and stems are of the same length. Vegetables with skins, such as aubergines, need to be pierced before microwaving to prevent bursting. It is always best to season vegetables with salt after cooking them.

Vegetable	Quantity	Approximate time on HIGH setting	Microwave Cooking Technique(s)
ARTICHOKE, GLOBE	1 2 3	5–6 minutes 7–8 minutes 11–12 minutes	*Place* upright in covered dish.
ASPARAGUS	350 g (12 oz)	5–7 minutes	*Place* stalks towards outside of dish. *Reposition* during cooking.
AUBERGINE	450 g (1 lb) sliced	8–10 minutes	*Stir* or *shake* after 4 minutes.
BEANS, BROAD	450 g (1 lb)	6–8 minutes	*Stir* or *shake* after 3 minutes and test after 5 minutes.
BEANS, GREEN	450 g (1 lb)	12–16 minutes	*Stir* or *shake* during cooking period. Time will vary with age and size.
BEETROOT, WHOLE	4 medium	14–16 minutes	*Pierce* skin with fork. *Reposition* during cooking.
BROCCOLI	450 g (1 lb)	10–12 minutes	*Reposition* during cooking. *Place* stalks towards outside of dish.
BRUSSELS SPROUTS	225 g (8 oz) 450 g (1 lb)	4–6 minutes 7–10 minutes	*Stir* or *shake* during cooking.
CABBAGE	450 g (1 lb) quartered or shredded	9–12 minutes	*Stir* or *shake* during cooking.
CARROTS	450 g (1 lb)	10–12 minutes	*Stir* or *shake* during cooking.
CAULIFLOWER	whole 225 g (8 oz) florets 450 g (1 lb) florets	12–16 minutes 7–8 minutes 10–12 minutes	*Stir* or *shake* during cooking.
CELERY	450 g (1 lb) sliced	7–10 minutes	*Stir* or *shake* during cooking.
CORN-ON-THE-COB	2	6–8 minutes	*Wrap* individually in greased greaseproof paper. *Do not* add water. *Turn* over after 3 minutes.
COURGETTES	450 g (1 lb) sliced	8–12 minutes	*Do not* add more than 30 ml (2 tbsp) water. *Stir* or *shake* gently twice during cooking. *Stand* for 2 minutes before draining.

Vegetable	Quantity	Approximate time on HIGH setting	Microwave Cooking Technique(s)
FENNEL	450 g (1 lb) sliced	9–10 minutes	*Stir* or *shake* during cooking.
LEEKS	450 g (1 lb) sliced	10–12 minutes	*Stir* of *shake* during cooking.
MUSHROOMS	225 g (8 oz)	2–3 minutes	*Do not* add water. Add 25 g (1 oz) butter and a squeeze of lemon juice. *Stir* or *shake* gently during cooking.
ONIONS	225 g (8 oz) sliced 175 g (6 oz) whole	4–6 minutes 10–12 minutes	*Stir* or *shake* sliced onions. *Add only* 60 ml (4 tbsp) water to whole onions. *Reposition* whole onions during cooking.
PARSNIPS	450 g (1 lb)	10–16 minutes	*Place* thinner parts towards centre. *Add* knob of butter and 15 ml (1 tbsp) lemon juice with 150 ml (¼ pint) water. *Turn* dish during cooking and *reposition*.
PEAS	450 g (1 lb)	9–11 minutes	*Stir* or *shake* during cooking.
POTATOES Baked jacket	1 x 175 g (6 oz) potato 2 x 175 g (6 oz) potatoes 4 x 175 g (6 oz) potatoes	4 minutes 6–8 minutes 12–14 minutes	*Wash* and prick skin with fork. *Place* on absorbent kitchen paper or napkin. When cooking more than 2 at a time, arrange in a circle. *Turn* over halfway through cooking.
Boiled (old)	450 g (1 lb)	7–10 minutes	*Stir* or *shake* during cooking.
Boiled (new)	450 g (1 lb)	6–8 minutes	*Do not* overcook or new potatoes become spongy.
Sweet	450 g (1 lb)	5 minutes	*Wash* and prick skin with fork. *Place* on absorbent kitchen paper. *Turn* over halfway through cooking time.
SPINACH	450 g (1 lb)	6–7 minutes	*Do not* add water. Best cooked in roasting bag, sealed with non-metal fastening. *Turn* dish during cooking.
SWEDE/TURNIP	450 g (1 lb) diced	10–15 minutes	*Stir* or *shake* during cooking.

Reheating

Food retains its flavour and colour when reheated in the microwave and there is no risk that it will stick to the pan.

Another advantage to reheating food in the microwave is, of course, the great time savings: many dishes take less than 1 minute to reheat, though times vary slightly depending on the starting temperature of the food; food straight from the refrigerator naturally takes longer than food at room temperature. With the microwave, there is no longer any need to keep pans of vegetables, sauces and meat for a late family diner – the entire main course can be reheated on one plate.

When arranging a meal on a plate, place dense, thick foods like meat towards the outside of the plate and thinner, porous foods like vegetables towards the centre.

Try to keep food in an even layer. Food can be stacked on plates in the microwave. Use an upturned soup plate for stacking, although special microwave stacking rings are best to use as they allow air to circulate underneath each plate; only the top plate must be covered. Arrange up to three plates on top of each other, but vertically alternate the meat and vegetables.

During reheating, food should be stirred or rotated. Cover dishes tightly and microwave on HIGH until the food is hot, though for best results, especially with stews, casseroles and frozen dishes, start on HIGH and switch to LOW for the second half of microwaving. Food is hot when the bottom of the container feels hot as the food will transfer some of its heat to the dish.

● Vegetables reheat very well, but fibrous vegetables like broccoli and asparagus are best reheated in a sauce as these vegetables toughen quickly. Always cover vegetables and slit boil-in-the-bags. Canned vegetables should be drained and transferred to a microwave container before reheating.

● Bread and pastry should be placed on absorbent kitchen paper during reheating to help absorb moisture. Pastry with sugary fillings such as mince pies will feel warm on the outside but the filling will be piping hot inside; during a few minutes standing time the heat will equalise. Do not leave the oven unattended while reheating these foods – a mince pie takes only 10 seconds to reheat.

● To help maintain the crispy base of pizza, brush the base with a little oil before reheating and place the pizza on a microwave rack to allow air to circulate, or reheat the pizza on a hot browning dish.

● Deep-fried foods become soggy if reheated.

● A Christmas pudding and other dense steamed puddings reheat so quickly that there is no time for them to develop their moist loose texture. For best results, arrange a single layer of slices of pudding in a circle with a glass of water in the centre. Microwave on HIGH until hot, then reshape pudding and flambé if liked.

MAKING DRINKS

Small quantities of water boil more quickly in a microwave than in the kettle, but for larger quantities a kettle will be much faster. It takes up to 10 minutes for 900 ml (1½ pints) water to boil in the microwave.

Milk-based drinks should be watched carefully as milk will boil over in the microwave just as easily as it does when heated in the conventional way. If a liquid starts to boil over, quickly open the door to stop microwave energy. Give liquids a good stir before microwaving them.

If heating more than 4 mugs of liquid, arrange them in a circle with spaces in between them and in the centre.

Coffee reheats superbly in the microwave. No need to waste left-over morning coffee. It will taste freshly brewed when reheated in the microwave.

Adapting recipes to the microwave

With an understanding of microwave cooking methods, it is not difficult to adapt your favourite recipes to the microwave. There is no need to be limited by specialized microwave cookbooks. Use these books to gain experience and then apply the techniques to your favourite recipes. In many cases only the containers and cooking times need to be changed.

ROASTING

Conventional roasting recipes are very simple to adapt to the microwave. Often it is simply a matter of consulting a microwave cooking chart to determine microwave time and setting. Remember that during standing the meat will continue to cook and the temperature on a meat thermometer will rise 5°C (9°F) – allow for this if using a probe and set the oven to switch off before it registers the temperature given in the recipe.

Small joints less than 1.4 kg (3 lb) do not have time to brown during microwaving. If you do not like the paler appearance of microwaved meats, completely cook them in the microwave, then glaze and brown the joint under the grill. Basting with juices that include paprika, turmeric, brown sugar, treacle or other dark-coloured flavouring will give the meat a slightly browned appearance. Alternatively, a small joint can be microwaved in a browning dish.

The joint is then left to stand, loosely covered or 'tented' with foil, and any gravy or sauce can then be made in the microwave oven.

GLAZED TURKEY ROLL WITH MUSTARD GRAVY

1.1 kg (2½ lb) rolled boneless turkey breast, ~~defrosted~~ if frozen

DEFROST ON LOW FOR 20-25 MINUTES THEN STAND FOR 1 HOUR.

30 ml (2 level tbsp) whole-grain mustard

30 ml (2 tbsp) thick honey

15 ml (1 tbsp) cornflour

300 ml (½ pt) chicken stock

salt and pepper

1 Place the turkey roll on a ~~rack set in a roasting tin and roast in the oven at 190°C (375°F) mark 5 for 1 hour~~.

MICROWAVE RACK IN MICROWAVE DISH AND MICROWAVE ON HIGH FOR 26 MINUTES.

2 Blend together the mustard and honey and brush half over the turkey. ~~Roast for a further 20 minutes~~, until the juices run clear when the meat is pierced in the centre with a metal skewer. Transfer the roast to a warmed serving dish and keep warm.

PLACE UNDER A HOT GRILL UNTIL GOLDEN BROWN.

3 Dissolve the cornflour in the stock and blend with the remaining mustard mixture. Season with salt and pepper. Add to the pan juices and ~~bring to the boil, stirring all the time, and cook until the gravy thickens.~~ Check seasoning.

MICROWAVE ON HIGH FOR 3 MINUTES, STIRRING OCCASIONALLY

4 Cut the turkey roll into thin slices and serve with the gravy handed separately.

Serves 4–6

GRILLING AND FRYING

Recipes for grilling and shallow or stir frying food – though not deep frying – can be successfully adapted to the microwave oven. Cook the food quickly in the microwave and then brown it under the grill. Alternatively, use a browning dish.

Many conventional recipes call for an initial frying to brown or sear meat before cooking. If you do not have a browning dish, brown conventionally and then cook the food in the microwave. Breadcrumb coatings, however, will not crisp in the microwave, even in a browning dish, because of steam rising from the food. When conventional recipes call for the food to be cooked under the grill, on the barbecue or shallow fried, use the microwave to partially cook the food and complete the dish conventionally.

FRIED SAUSAGES WITH PEPPERS

REDUCE TO 15 ml. (1 tbsp.) OIL.

30 ml (2 tbsp) vegetable oil

450 g (1 lb) pork sausages

2 medium onions, skinned and thinly sliced

half a red pepper, seeded and sliced into rings

half a green pepper, seeded and sliced into rings

1 green eating apple, cored and sliced

salt

pinch of paprika

1 Heat the oil in a frying pan and fry the sausages until brown all over. Remove the sausages with a slotted spoon and keep warm.

BROWN THE SAUSAGES UNDER A CONVENTIONAL GRILL. ALTERNATIVELY, HEAT A BROWNING DISH ACCORDING TO MANUFACTURER'S INSTRUCTIONS. ADD THE OIL DURING THE LAST 30 SECONDS OF HEATING, THEN BROWN THE SAUSAGES

PLACE IN A MEDIUM BOWL WITH THE OIL AND MICROWAVE ON HIGH FOR 5 MINUTES OR UNTIL SOFT, STIRRING ONCE.

2 Add the onions and peppers to the fat remaining in the pan and cook for 5 minutes, stirring occasionally.

3 Return the sausages to the pan, add the apple slices and cook for 3–4 minutes. Season with salt and paprika and serve at once.

Serves 4

ADD THE SAUSAGES AND APPLE TO THE BOWL AND MICROWAVE ON HIGH FOR 2 MINUTES OR UNTIL COOKED.

STEWING AND BRAISING

Conventionally cooked stews and casseroles depend on long, slow cooking to tenderise tough cuts of meat and for flavours of vegetables and herbs to combine. For this reason, there is little point in using the microwave for any stews other than those with ingredients which do not need tenderising such as most poultry and vegetable stews.

When adapting conventional casserole or stew recipes to the microwave, it is usually necessary to reduce the amount of liquid as there is less evaporation when microwaving. Start with about one-quarter less liquid and add more during cooking if necessary. Herbs and spices, especially strong-flavoured ones, do not have time to mellow so use less than stated in conventional recipes.

SPANISH CHICKEN IN RED WINE

REDUCE TO 15ml. (1tbsp.) OIL.

30 ml (2 tbsp) vegetable oil

4 chicken pieces

125 g (4 oz) bacon rashers, rinded and chopped

225 g (8 oz) button mushrooms, wiped

45 ml (3 level tbsp) plain flour

REDUCE TO 150ml. (¼ PINT) WINE.

300 ml (½ pint) red wine

salt and pepper

OMIT.

150 ml (¼ pint) chicken stock

50 g (2 oz) green olives, stoned

1 Heat the oil in a frying pan and brown the chicken pieces on both sides. Transfer the chicken to a casserole dish.

HEAT A BROWNING DISH ACCORDING TO MANUFACTURER'S INSTRUCTIONS, ADDING THE OIL FOR THE LAST 30 SECONDS. ADD THE CHICKEN AND QUICKLY BROWN.

2 Add the bacon and mushrooms and cook for 2–3 minutes. Stir in the flour and cook, stirring, for 1 minute. Gradually stir in the red wine and stock and bring to the boil. Season to taste.

MICROWAVE ON HIGH FOR 2 MINUTES.

MICROWAVE ON HIGH FOR 30 SECONDS.

OMIT.

3 Pour the sauce over the chicken and add the olives. Cover and cook in the oven at 180°C (350°F) mark 4 for about 1 hour or until the chicken is tender.

MICROWAVE ON HIGH FOR 5 MINUTES OR UNTIL BOILING, STIRRING OCCASIONALLY.

COVER AND MICROWAVE ON HIGH FOR 10 MINUTES. TURN CHICKEN OVER AND MICROWAVE, UNCOVERED, ON HIGH FOR 8 MINUTES OR UNTIL CHICKEN IS TENDER.

Serves 4

POACHING, STEAMING AND BOILING

When cooking conventionally these cooking methods require added liquid to help tenderise food and retain its moisture, to rehydrate it (as with rice) or simply to prevent food from sticking to the pan. Because microwaved food cooks in its own moisture and there is no risk of sticking, the amount of liquid added is minimal, often much less than the liquid indicated in a conventional recipe. When steaming foods, added liquid is eliminated altogether and most fresh vegetables can be microwaved in less than 90 ml (6 tbsp) water. Very moist vegetables such as corn-on-the-cob and spinach require no added water. With all these forms of cooking the container should be three-quarters covered to allow steam to escape; steamed puddings should be completely but loosely covered.

In most cases cooking times are greatly reduced. The exceptions are rice and dried pasta because they need to rehydrate before they start cooking. Therefore, they require the same cooking time as a conventional recipe.

LAYFAYETTE PUDDING

125 g (4 oz) self-raising flour

75 g (3 oz) ground almonds

50 g (2 oz) fresh white breadcrumbs

125 g (4 oz) butter

125 g (4 oz) granulated sugar

2 eggs, beaten

50 g (2 oz) glacé cherries, chopped

45 ml (3 tbsp) milk

egg custard sauce, to serve (page 117)

1 Grease a 900 ml (1½ pint) pudding basin.

2 Mix together the flour, ground almonds and breadcrumbs.

3 Cream the butter and sugar together until pale and fluffy. Add the eggs a little at a time, beating well after each addition. Fold in half the flour mixture with a metal spoon, then fold in the remainder along with the cherries and milk to give a dropping consistency.

4 Spoon the mixture into the basin, ~~cover with greased greaseproof paper and foil~~ and secure in place with string.

COVER VERY LOOSELY WITH CLING FILM TO ALLOW SPACE FOR THE PUDDING TO RISE.

MICROWAVE ON HIGH FOR 4½ MINUTES. LEAVE TO STAND, COVERED, FOR 5 MINUTES.

5 ~~Place the basin in a steamer or large, heavy-based saucepan and pour in enough boiling water to come halfway up the sides of the basin. Cover the pan and steam the pudding for 1½–2 hours, until well risen and firm to the touch.~~

6 Turn the pudding out on to a warmed serving dish and serve with custard.

Serves 4–6

Vegetable terrine (Eggs and Cheese) *opposite*

BAKING

Follow recipe instructions for greasing and lining but do not grease and flour containers as this produces a soggy coating to the cake. Instead, use greased greaseproof paper. As most conventional baking equipment is made of metal, choose from the wide range of containers which can be placed in the microwave such as ovenglass and plastic containers (which do not need to be greased).

Microwaved cakes will rise higher during cooking than those conventionally baked. To avoid possible spillage, never fill a container more than half-full.

When calculating cooking times in the microwave your best guide is to compare the ingredients and method used in a conventional recipe and follow the microwave cooking time. Make sure the cake is given quarter turns. When cooked, a cake will look firm or dry on top and will have pulled away slightly from the sides of the container. Leave cakes in the container for the time given in the recipe but once turned out, quickly remove paper.

WALNUT APPLE CAKE

175 g (6 oz) butter, ~~softened~~

175 g (6 oz) dark soft brown sugar

MICROWAVE ON LOW FOR 20-30 SECONDS OR UNTIL SOFT.

2 eggs

30 ml (2 tbsp) milk

275 g (10 oz) self-raising wholemeal flour

2.5 ml (½ tsp) ground cinnamon

125 g (4 oz) seedless raisins or sultanas

225 g (8 oz) cooking apple, peeled, cored and grated

50 g (2 oz) walnuts, chopped

finely grated rind and juice of 1 lemon

100 g (4 oz) icing sugar, sifted

8 walnuts, to decorate

1 Grease and line a 20.5 cm (8 inch) deep round ~~cake tin.~~

NOTE METHOD IN WHICH INGREDIENTS ARE COMBINED AND COMPARE WITH A MICROWAVE RECIPE TO CALCULATE COOKING TIME. THIS IS A CREAMED MIXTURE.

2 Cream the butter and sugar together until pale and fluffy, then gradually beat in the eggs and milk. Stir in the flour, cinnamon, fruit and chopped nuts. Mix well and spoon into the tin.

USE OVENGLASS, SOUFFLE DISH OR OTHER, NON-METAL DEEP DISH AND BASE-LINE WITH GREASED, GREASE-PROOF PAPER.

3 ~~Bake in the oven at 190°C (375°F) mark 5 for 25-30 minutes.~~ Leave to cool in the tin, then turn out on to a wire rack and leave until cold; peel off the paper.

MICROWAVE ON MEDIUM FOR 20 MINUTES.

4 Combine the lemon rind and juice with the icing sugar to give a pouring consistency. Spread the icing over the cake and decorate with walnuts.

Makes 6–8 slices

Tagliatelle with smoked ham and peas
(Pasta) *opposite*

Meal planning using the microwave

Effective utilisation of time is the secret of a successful dinner party and a microwave oven can be tremendously helpful in this respect. The meal can be cooked or partially prepared in advance, so the cook has more time to spend with guests.

One distinct advantage of a microwave is that food can be served directly from the dish in which it was cooked, thus there are no serving dishes to be warmed before the meal and less washing up after it.

A freezer/microwave combination can take all the hard work out of entertaining. When cooking certain dishes such as casseroles, pies and bolognese sauce for spaghetti or lasagne, cook double the recipe and freeze the remainder to reheat for a last minute dinner party.

To help you see how to best organise your time when cooking for a dinner party or the family, we have devised the following menus with step-by-step instructions giving the order of these preparations, so that no time is wasted.

FAMILY SUPPER FOR FOUR

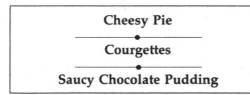

Cheesy Pie
•
Courgettes
•
Saucy Chocolate Pudding

On the day of serving

Prepare and cook the Cheesy Pie (page 47).

About 40 minutes before serving

Prepare the Chocolate Pudding (page 104) to the end of stage 3.

Prepare and cook the courgettes: slice 450 g (1 lb) courgettes and place in a serving dish with 30 ml (2 tbsp) water. Cover and microwave on HIGH for 8–10 minutes. Leave to stand, covered.

While vegetables are standing, reheat the Cheesy Pie on HIGH for 5 minutes.

Just before serving

Finish making the Chocolate Pudding: cook in the microwave while eating the main course.

DINNER PARTY FOR SIX

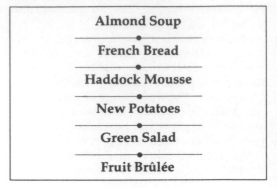

Almond Soup
•
French Bread
•
Haddock Mousse
•
New Potatoes
•
Green Salad
•
Fruit Brûlée

The day before

Make the Fruit Brûlée (page 100) to the end of stage 4. Chill overnight.

Make the Haddock Mousse (page 60) to the end of stage 7. Chill overnight.

Make the Almond Soup (page 37) to the end of stage 3. Cover and refrigerate. Toast the flaked almonds for the soup: place them on a large plate and microwave on HIGH for 10 minutes or until golden brown, stirring occasionally. Wrap and store in an airtight tin.

The day of serving

Finish making the Fruit Brûlée, allowing at least 1 hour for chilling.

About 40 minutes before serving

Prepare the potatoes: wash and scrub 700 g (1½ lb) new potatoes, cut in half if necessary and place them in a roasting bag with 30 ml (2 tbsp) water and a sprig of mint, if liked.

Unmould the Haddock Mousse on to a serving dish.

Prepare the green salad.

Just before serving

Reheat the Almond soup on HIGH for 4–5 minutes or until hot and continue with stage 4 of recipe.

To serve

Garnish the soup with the toasted almonds and serve with French bread.

During the first course, cook the potatoes in the microwave on HIGH for 10 minutes.

Spoon a little of the mayonnaise over the Haddock Mousse, garnish and serve with the potatoes and salad. Serve the dessert.

RECIPES
FOR THE
MICROWAVE
OVEN

Good Housekeeping have developed and tested over
150 delicious new recipes which take full advantage
of microwave cooking. We have emphasised those
dishes which adapt well to microwave cooking and
tell you at a glance which recipes require both
conventional and microwave cooking. Nothing is left
to chance with microwave cooking so we give you
exact cooking times and complete instructions in an
easy-to-follow format along with a number of helpful
tips to make cooking easier.

Soups and starters

Soups and many starters can be prepared quickly and if necessary, reheated just before serving.

Soups

Because most stocks require long slow simmering to bring out flavour, they are best made in the conventional way, especially beef stocks which depend on tough cuts of meat for flavour. However, small quantities of fish, vegetable and chicken stocks can be successfully made in the microwave in the same way that soups are made. Use less water than usual as there is less evaporation when microwaving. For best results, make the stock in advance and refrigerate overnight to give flavours a chance to develop and mellow.

Vegetables for soups will cook quickly and because they retain their natural colours, soups will be brighter; herbs will also not discolour in the microwave. For hearty soups, cook pasta and pulses in the conventional way and add to soups towards the end of cooking time. Canned pulses, which are ready-cooked, need only to be drained and added to the soup.

When adding cream or a liaison of cream and egg yolk to soups, stir in after microwaving the puréed soup mixture to reheat it; the heat of the purée will be sufficient to heat the cream or to incorporate the liaison. If necessary, gently reheat a cream-based soup on LOW. Remember, single cream, soured cream and yogurt separate if they are allowed to boil.

Soups actually improve in flavour when made in advance in the microwave and then reheated. Their flavours have a chance to mellow if refrigerated for several hours and then reheated. Reheat soups, including canned soups, in the serving bowl or mugs. Reheat on HIGH unless cream or egg have been added. Stir the soup as soon as it starts to bubble around the edges, then continue microwaving on HIGH until bubbles form again, stir and serve. Reheat soups from frozen. Remove the carton or bag as soon as possible, break up the soup and three-quarters cover with cling film. Reheat on HIGH, stirring to break up any lumps.

Dehydrated soups should be soaked in the required amount of water for about 30 minutes to soften. They can then be microwaved on HIGH until boiling and then left to stand for a few minutes.

Starters

Many starters require last-minute preparation and for those served hot the microwave can be of great help. Prepare individual gratin dishes in advance and reheat in the microwave, then brown under a hot grill. Use the microwave to quickly cook vegetables, either microwave a tasty vegetable filling or cook vegetables to be served cold.

Remember that bread can be warmed and toast reheated in the microwave. Butter for spreading can be softened on LOW in 1 minute.

Almond Soup

TIMES		METHOD	SETTINGS	SERVINGS
PREP. 20	COOK 18	MICRO.	HIGH	6

100 g (4 oz) ground almonds

2 celery sticks, trimmed and finely chopped

1 small onion, skinned and finely chopped

600 ml (1 pint) chicken stock

25 g (1 oz) butter or margarine

25 g (1 oz) plain flour

300 ml (½ pint) milk

45 ml (3 tbsp) double cream

1 egg yolk

salt and pepper

toasted flaked almonds, to garnish

1 Mix the almonds, celery and onion together in a large bowl and pour in the stock. Cover and microwave on HIGH for 10 minutes or until boiling, then microwave for a further 4 minutes.

2 Strain the liquid through a sieve and rub the almond paste through using a wooden spoon.

3 Place the butter or margarine in the rinsed-out bowl and microwave on HIGH for 45 seconds or until melted. Stir in the flour and microwave on HIGH for 30 seconds. Gradually whisk in the milk and almond liquid and microwave on HIGH for 3 minutes or until boiling.

4 Blend the cream and egg yolk together and slowly add to the soup, stirring until well blended. Season to taste with salt and pepper. Garnish with the toasted almonds and serve.

Celery and Stilton Soup

TIMES		METHOD	SETTINGS	SERVINGS
PREP. 10	COOK 16	MICRO.	HIGH	6

25 g (1 oz) butter or margarine

4 celery sticks, trimmed and finely chopped

30 ml (2 level tbsp) plain flour

300 ml (½ pint) milk

600 ml (1 pint) chicken stock

225 g (8 oz) Stilton cheese, crumbled

salt and pepper

1 Place the butter or margarine in a large serving bowl and microwave on HIGH for 45 seconds or until melted. Stir in the celery, cover, and microwave on HIGH for 5 minutes or until the celery begins to soften.

2 Stir in the flour and microwave on HIGH for 30 seconds. Gradually stir in the milk and stock. Cover and microwave on HIGH for 8 minutes or until the celery is tender. Stir occasionally during cooking.

3 Gradually add the Stilton and stir until well blended with the liquid. Season to taste, adding salt carefully as Stilton can be rather salty.

4 Heat through in the microwave on HIGH for 1–2 minutes. Serve immediately.

COOK'S TIP

Serve with warmed bread rolls. Place 4 rolls in a wicker serving basket and microwave on HIGH for 20–30 seconds.

Minted Courgette Soup

TIMES PREP	COOK	METHOD	SETTINGS	SERVINGS
25	15	MICRO.	HIGH	6

450 g (1 lb) courgettes

1 bunch of spring onions, trimmed

25 g (1 oz) butter or margarine

900 ml (1½ pints) chicken stock

45 ml (3 tbsp) chopped fresh mint

salt and pepper

142 g (5 oz) natural yogurt

yogurt and fresh mint sprigs, to garnish

1 Trim and thinly slice the courgettes. Thinly slice the spring onions.

2 Place the butter or margarine in a large bowl and microwave on HIGH for 45 seconds or until melted. Add the courgettes and onions. Cover and microwave on HIGH for 6 minutes, or until the courgettes are beginning to soften.

3 Stir in the stock and mint and season to taste with salt and pepper. Microwave on HIGH for 8 minutes or until the vegetables are soft.

4 Purée the soup in a blender or food processor and leave to cool. Add the yogurt and stir well. Check seasoning and chill.

5 Ladle the soup into individual chilled bowls. Garnish each bowl with a swirl of yogurt and a mint sprig. Serve immediately.

COOK'S TIP

This soup is also excellent served hot. Reheat the soup after puréeing in stage 4, then stir in the yogurt and heat through without boiling. Garnish with mint and serve.

Tomato and Carrot Soup

TIMES PREP	COOK	METHOD	SETTINGS	SERVINGS
30	27	MICRO.	HIGH	6

25 g (1 oz) butter or margarine

1 large onion, skinned and finely chopped

1 garlic clove, skinned and crushed

225 g (8 oz) carrots, peeled and finely chopped

450 g (1 lb) ripe tomatoes, skinned and chopped

2 eating apples, peeled, cored and diced

1 bouquet garni

1.1 litres (2 pints) chicken stock

salt and pepper

double cream and snipped chives, to garnish

1 Place the butter or margarine in a large bowl and microwave on HIGH for 45 seconds or until melted. Stir in the onion and garlic. Cover and microwave on HIGH for 3 minutes or until the onion begins to soften.

2 Add the carrots, tomatoes, apples, bouquet garni and stock. Season to taste, cover and microwave on HIGH for 21 minutes or until the vegetables are tender.

3 Discard the bouquet garni and purée the mixture in a blender or food processor. Pour the soup back into the bowl and microwave on HIGH for 2 minutes or until hot.

4 Ladle the soup into warmed bowls and swirl the tops with double cream. Sprinkle with chives and serve.

Potato and Onion Soup

TIMES		METHOD	SETTINGS	SERVINGS
PREP.	COOK	MICRO.	HIGH	6
20	27			

40 g (1½ oz) butter or margarine

1 bunch of spring onions, trimmed and chopped

450 g (1 lb) potatoes, peeled and diced

1 bay leaf

600 ml (1 pint) chicken stock

salt and pepper

150 ml (¼ pint) milk

90 ml (6 tbsp) double cream

strips of spring onion, to garnish

1 Place the butter or margarine in a large serving bowl and microwave on HIGH for 45 seconds or until melted. Add the spring onions, cover and microwave on HIGH for 5–7 minutes or until soft.

2 Add the potatoes, bay leaf, stock and seasoning and microwave on HIGH for 15 minutes or until the vegetables are tender. Discard the bay leaf.

3 Leave to cool slightly, then purée in a blender or food processor.

4 Pour the soup back into the bowl, add the milk and reheat on HIGH for 4 minutes. Add the cream and whisk thoroughly. Check seasoning. Garnish with strips of spring onion.

COOK'S TIP

Make sure to use the green tops from the spring onions to give the soup a good colour.

Lentil and Bacon Soup

TIMES		METHOD	SETTINGS	SERVINGS
PREP.	COOK	MICRO.	HIGH	6
25	23			

125 g (4 oz) streaky bacon, rinded and chopped

25 g (1 oz) butter or margarine

100 g (4 oz) red lentils

2 leeks, trimmed, washed and finely chopped

2 carrots, peeled and finely chopped

1 litre (1¾ pints) chicken stock

30 ml (2 tbsp) chopped fresh parsley

salt and pepper

orange shreds, to garnish

1 Place the bacon and butter or margarine in a large bowl and microwave on HIGH for 2 minutes. Add the lentils and toss to coat them in the fat, then add the leeks, carrots and stock.

2 Cover and microwave on HIGH for 18 minutes or until the lentils are cooked. Stir two or three times during the cooking time.

3 Cool slightly, then purée the soup in a blender or food processor. Add the parsley, season and microwave on HIGH for 2–3 minutes or until hot. Garnish with orange shreds and serve.

Smoked Haddock Chowder

TIMES		METHOD	SETTINGS	SERVINGS
PREP.	COOK	MICRO.	HIGH	4
15	14			

450 g (1 lb) smoked haddock fillet

1 bay leaf

450 ml (¾ pint) milk

25 g (1 oz) butter or margarine

1 large floury potato, peeled and finely diced

10 ml (2 tsp) lemon juice

chopped fresh parsley, to garnish

1 Place the fish in a shallow dish with the bay leaf. Pour over the milk. Cover and microwave on HIGH for 7 minutes or until cooked, turning the dish once.

2 Drain, reserving the cooking liquid. Flake the fish, discarding the skin and any bones. Set aside.

3 Place the butter or margarine and diced potato in a large serving bowl. Cover and microwave on HIGH for 5 minutes or until the potato begins to soften.

4 Add the fish, reserved cooking liquid, lemon juice, and 150 ml (¼ pint) water. Stir gently and microwave on HIGH for 2 minutes or until heated through. Garnish with parsley and serve.

Mussel Bisque

TIMES		METHOD	SETTINGS	SERVINGS
PREP.	COOK	MICRO	HIGH	6
8	9			

25 g (1 oz) butter or margarine

30 ml (2 level tbsp) plain flour

900 ml (1½ pints) milk

60 ml (4 tbsp) dry sherry

450 g (1 lb) frozen mussels, thawed

150 ml (5 fl oz) single cream

salt and pepper

chopped fresh parsley, to garnish

1 Place the butter or margarine in a large serving bowl and microwave on HIGH for 45 seconds or until melted.

2 Stir in the flour and microwave on HIGH for 30 seconds. Gradually whisk in the milk and the sherry. Microwave on HIGH for 4 minutes, whisking after every minute, until the sauce is boiling and has thickened.

3 Add the mussels and microwave on HIGH for 2–4 minutes or until mussels are heated through. Stir in the single cream and season. Serve, garnished with chopped parsley.

COOK'S TIP

Use three 142 g (5 oz) jars of mussels, drained and rinsed, instead of the frozen mussels.

Mushrooms in Garlic Butter

TIMES		METHOD	SETTINGS	SERVINGS
PREP.	COOK	MICRO.	HIGH	4
15	11			

225 g (8 oz) medium mushrooms, wiped

50 g (2 oz) butter or margarine

2 garlic cloves, skinned and crushed

1 small onion, skinned and finely chopped

15 g (½ oz) fresh brown breadcrumbs

30 ml (2 tbsp) chopped fresh parsley

salt and pepper

1 Remove the mushroom stems and finely chop them. Set the mushroom caps aside.

2 Place the butter or margarine in a medium bowl and microwave on HIGH for 45 seconds or until melted. Add the garlic, onion and chopped mushroom stems. Cover and microwave on HIGH for 5–7 minutes or until soft. Stir in the breadcrumbs, parsley and seasoning.

3 Stuff each mushroom cap with a little of the mixture, pressing down lightly. Arrange the mushrooms in a circle on a plate and microwave on HIGH for 2–3 minutes, or until hot.

Serve with French bread.

Leeks à la Grecque

TIMES		METHOD	SETTINGS	SERVINGS
PREP.	COOK	MICRO.	HIGH	6
20	16			

6 medium sized leeks

1 small onion, skinned and finely chopped

2 large tomatoes, skinned, seeded and chopped

100 ml (4 fl oz) dry white wine

75 ml (3 tbsp) olive oil

1 garlic clove, skinned and crushed

salt and pepper

chopped fresh basil or parsley, to garnish

1 Remove the tough outer leaves from the leeks and trim the bases and tops. Slice lengthways and wash well under cold running water. Cut into 5 cm (2 inch) lengths.

2 Place in a shallow dish in a single layer. Sprinkle over the onion and tomatoes. Add the wine, oil and garlic. Season to taste with salt and pepper. Cover and microwave on HIGH for 13–16 minutes or until the leeks are tender.

3 Leave until cold. Serve on side plates garnished with the basil or parsley.

Serve with hot crusty bread and butter.

COOK'S TIP

To ensure that the leeks cook evenly, make sure they are all the same thickness and are cut into even-sized lengths.

Curried Eggs

TIMES PREP / COOK	METHOD	SETTINGS	SERVINGS
15 / 19	MICRO. CONVEN.	HIGH	6

6 eggs

1 medium onion, skinned and finely chopped

15 ml (1 tbsp) vegetable oil

10 ml (2 level tsp) curry powder

5 ml (1 level tsp) paprika

10 ml (2 level tsp) tomato purée

150 ml (¼ pint) mayonnaise

142 g (5 oz) natural yogurt

watercress, to garnish

1 Conventionally boil the eggs for 10 minutes starting with cold water. Drain and rinse under cold running water to arrest further cooking. Shell, and cut the eggs in half lengthways.

2 Mix the onion and oil together in a small bowl and microwave on HIGH for 5–7 minutes or until the onion has softened.

3 Stir in the curry powder, paprika and tomato purée. Microwave on HIGH for 2 minutes. Cool slightly, then add the mayonnaise and yogurt.

4 Arrange the halved eggs cut side down on individual serving plates. Pour over the curry sauce and garnish with watercress.

Serve with thinly sliced brown bread and butter.

Crabmeat-Filled Courgette Slices

TIMES PREP / COOK	METHOD	SETTINGS	SERVINGS
15 / 11	MICRO. CONVEN.	HIGH	4

4 medium courgettes

150 g (5 oz) can crabmeat, drained and flaked

50 g (2 oz) fresh breadcrumbs

10 ml (2 tsp) lemon juice

60 ml (4 tbsp) soured cream or mayonnaise

15 ml (1 tbsp) snipped chives

60 ml (4 level tbsp) freshly grated Parmesan cheese

salt and pepper

fresh chives, to garnish

1 Trim the courgettes and cut in half lengthways. Using a teaspoon, scoop out the centres to make a small hollow. Discard the centres.

2 Put the courgette halves into a shallow flameproof dish with 45 ml (3 tbsp) water. Cover and microwave on HIGH for 5 minutes.

3 Meanwhile, mix the crabmeat, breadcrumbs, lemon juice, soured cream or mayonnaise, chives and half the Parmesan cheese together. Season to taste with salt and pepper.

4 Pour off the liquid from the dish of courgettes. Divide the crabmeat mixture between each courgette, neatly stuffing along the centres. Sprinkle with the remaining Parmesan cheese. Cover and microwave on HIGH for 4 minutes or until hot.

5 Brown the cheese topping under a hot grill. Garnish with fresh chives and serve.

This filling starter needs no accompaniment.

Farmhouse Pâté

TIMES		METHOD	SETTINGS	SERVINGS
PREP	COOK	MICRO.	LOW	8
30	25			

225 g (8 oz) lamb's liver, coarsely chopped

700 g (1½ lb) belly of pork, rinded and coarsely chopped

1 large onion, skinned and chopped

1 garlic clove, skinned and crushed

60 ml (4 level tbsp) tomato purée

30 ml (2 tbsp) brandy

50 g (2 oz) stuffed green olives, sliced

2.5 ml (½ level tsp) mixed herbs

salt and pepper

225 g (8 oz) streaky bacon, rinded

1 Mince the liver, pork, onion and garlic together in a mincer or food processor.

2 Place in a bowl and mix in the tomato purée, brandy, olives and herbs. Season to taste with salt and pepper.

3 Line a terrine dish with the streaky bacon rashers and spoon in the liver mixture.

4 Cover and microwave on LOW for 25 minutes. Cool in the dish, then refrigerate overnight.

5 Turn out, and serve cut in slices.

Serve with hot buttered toast.

Smoked Fish Pâté

TIMES		METHOD	SETTINGS	SERVINGS
PREP	COOK	MICRO.	HIGH	4
7	7			

350 g (12 oz) smoked haddock fillet

1 small lemon

75 g (3 oz) butter or margarine

5 ml (1 tsp) snipped chives

pepper

1 Place the fish in a shallow dish with 60 ml (4 tbsp) water. Cover and microwave on HIGH for 6 minutes or until tender. Drain well. Remove the skin and flake the fish, discarding any bones.

2 Cut 4 slices from the lemon. Finely grate the rind and squeeze the juice from the remaining lemon.

3 Place the butter or margarine in a medium bowl and microwave on HIGH for 45 seconds or until melted. Stir in the flaked haddock, lemon rind, lemon juice and chives. Season with pepper and mix well together.

4 Divide the pâté equally between four ramekin dishes. Cover and chill in the refrigerator for at least 4 hours. Garnish with the lemon slices and serve.

Serve with Melba toast or hot buttered toast.

COOK'S TIP

To make Melba toast, toast the bread on both sides, then using a sharp knife, slice the bread in half horizontally. Place untoasted side up on a microwave baking sheet or large plate and microwave on HIGH for 30–40 seconds until dry and crisp.

Eggs and Cheese

Eggs and cheese are good to have on hand for making a number of tasty lunch, supper and main dishes. Eggs and most cheeses are high in fat which attracts microwaves so they cook quickly. But because eggs can curdle and cheese will separate, they must be carefully cooked. Remember that eggs and cheese continue cooking after microwaving has stopped.

Eggs

Eggs cannot be boiled in the microwave because pressure builds up under the shell causing the egg to burst. Nor should eggs be reheated as they can turn rubbery.

Other methods of cooking eggs are very successful in the microwave. When poaching eggs, the yolk, which is surrounded by a membrane, should be gently pricked before cooking to help prevent it from bursting. Use a skewer or the prongs of a fork – if the yolk oozes this means it has been pricked too deeply. Poach eggs in a special microwave muffin pan or bun tray – they can be cooked without adding water or fat to the pan. The yolk, which contains the fat in eggs, will cook before the white.

Scrambled eggs are lighter and fluffier when microwaved because there is less evaporation of liquid than there is when eggs are scrambled in the conventional way and there are no crusty pans to clean up afterwards. They can be made on a serving plate or in a small bowl without adding fat. Fried eggs can be made in a preheated browning dish, but there is no time saving because of the time needed to preheat the dish.

A number of egg dishes can be partially made in the microwave. Cook a sauce for hard-boiled eggs in the microwave or for a traditional English breakfast, fry the eggs in the conventional way and cook the bacon or sausages in the microwave.

Cheese

Cheese melts rapidly in the microwave and care should be taken that it does not toughen and separate. Usually cheese is stirred into a white sauce and this can be done very successfully – remove the sauce from the microwave and melt the cheese in the heat of the sauce. For cheese toppings, which look most attractive when browned, a conventional grill should be used. Cook casseroles in the microwave, cover with a cheese and breadcrumb topping and finish off under the grill.

Eggs Florentine

TIMES		METHOD	SETTINGS	SERVINGS
PREP	COOK	MICRO.	HIGH	4
30	14	CONVEN.		

900 g (2 lb) fresh spinach, washed and trimmed

25 g (1 oz) butter or margarine

45 ml (3 level tbsp) plain flour

1.25 ml (¼ level tsp) mustard powder

300 ml (½ pint) milk

100 g (4 oz) Cheddar cheese, finely grated

salt and pepper

4 eggs

1 Coarsely chop the spinach and place in a large bowl. Cover and microwave on HIGH for 4 minutes or until just tender. Leave to stand, covered.

2 Place the butter or margarine in a medium bowl and microwave on HIGH for 45 seconds or until melted. Stir in the flour and mustard and microwave on HIGH for 30 seconds, then gradually whisk in the milk. Microwave on HIGH for 5 minutes, or until boiling and thickened, whisking after every minute. Stir in two-thirds of the cheese. Season to taste.

3 Break the eggs into a microwave muffin pan or bun tray. Gently prick the yolks with a skewer and microwave on HIGH for 2 minutes or until just set.

4 Drain the spinach thoroughly, place in a flameproof dish, top with the eggs and spoon over the sauce. Sprinkle with the reserved cheese and brown under a hot grill.

Serve with brown bread and butter.

Eggs Benedict

TIMES		METHOD	SETTINGS	SERVINGS
PREP	COOK	MICRO.	HIGH	3
15	6	CONVEN.		

3 English muffins, split

150 g (5 oz) unsalted butter

3 thin slices of cooked ham, halved

6 eggs

For the sauce:

3 egg yolks

30 ml (2 tbsp) lemon juice

salt and pepper

1 Grill the muffins on the split sides until golden brown. Spread with 25 g (1 oz) of the butter. Top each muffin with half a slice of ham and keep warm.

2 Break the eggs into a microwave muffin pan or bun tray. Gently prick each yolk and microwave on HIGH for 2½ minutes or until just set.

3 To make the sauce, beat the egg yolks, lemon juice, salt and pepper together in a small bowl.

4 Cut the remaining butter into quarters and place in a medium bowl. Microwave on HIGH for 45 seconds or until melted. Stir in the egg yolk mixture and whisk thoroughly with a balloon whisk. Microwave on HIGH for 45 seconds or until the sauce is just thick enough to coat the back of a spoon, whisking every 15 seconds during cooking.

5 Remove from the oven and continue to whisk the sauce for about 20 seconds to thicken further.

6 To serve, place an egg on top of each ham-topped muffin and spoon over the sauce.

Advance preparation: the sauce can be made in advance and kept in the refrigerator; cover the surface with cling flim to prevent a skin forming. Reheat on LOW and whisk often, otherwise the sauce may curdle. If the sauce starts to curdle, quickly open the oven door and whisk the sauce vigorously.

Egg Fricassee

TIMES		METHOD	SETTINGS	SERVINGS
PREP. 10	COOK 19	MICRO. CONVEN.	HIGH	4

200 ml (7 fl oz) milk

small slice of onion

half a small carrot, sliced

1 bay leaf

6 black peppercorns

6 eggs

25 g (1 oz) butter or margarine

30 ml (2 level tbsp) plain flour

142 ml (5 fl oz) soured cream

30 ml (2 tbsp) snipped chives or finely chopped fresh tarragon

salt and pepper

boiled rice, to serve

1 Pour the milk into a measuring jug and add the onion, carrot, bay leaf and peppercorns. Microwave on HIGH for 3 minutes or until boiling. Leave to stand, covered, for 15 minutes.

2 Meanwhile, conventionally boil the eggs for 10 minutes starting with cold water. Rinse under cold running water, shell and cut into slices. Keep the eggs warm.

3 Strain the milk discarding the vegetables, bay leaf and peppercorns.

4 Place the butter or margarine in a medium bowl and microwave on HIGH for 45 seconds or until melted. Stir in the flour and microwave on HIGH for 30 seconds. Gradually whisk in the milk and microwave on HIGH for 5 minutes or until boiling and thickened, whisking occasionally. Whisk in the soured cream and chives or tarragon. Season to taste.

5 Reserve a few egg slices and add the rest to the sauce. Garnish with the egg slices and serve at once with rice.

Advance preparation: the sauce can be made in advance and reheated, but do not allow it to boil. Add the eggs just before serving; they should not be reheated with the sauce or they may become rubbery.

Scrambled Eggs with Smoked Haddock

TIMES		METHOD	SETTINGS	SERVINGS
PREP. 10	COOK 6	MICRO.	HIGH	2

100 g (4 oz) smoked haddock fillet

25 g (1 oz) butter or margarine

4 eggs

60 ml (4 tbsp) milk

salt and pepper

2 slices of hot buttered toast, to serve

1 Place the fish in a shallow dish with 30 ml (2 tbsp) water. Cover and microwave on HIGH for 3 minutes or until tender.

2 Drain the fish and remove the skin. Flake the flesh, discarding any bones. Keep hot.

3 In a medium bowl, microwave the butter or margarine on HIGH for 45 seconds or until melted.

4 Beat the eggs and milk together with a fork and stir into the melted fat. Microwave on HIGH for 1–2 minutes or until just set, stirring once or twice. Quickly stir in the fish and season to taste with salt and pepper. Serve immediately on slices of toast.

Cheese Soufflé

TIMES PREP.	COOK	METHOD	SETTINGS	SERVINGS
15	14	MICRO.	LOW / HIGH	4

40 g (1½ oz) butter or margarine
25 g (1 oz) plain flour
140 ml (5 fl oz) milk
2.5 ml (½ level tsp) mustard powder
salt and pepper
3 eggs, separated
75 g (3 oz) mature Cheddar cheese, finely grated

1 Rub the inside of a 1.4 litre (2½ pint) soufflé dish with 15 g (½ oz) butter or margarine.

2 Place the remaining butter or margarine in a medium bowl and microwave on HIGH for 45 seconds or until melted. Stir in the flour and microwave on HIGH for 30 seconds. Using a balloon whisk, gradually whisk in the milk, mustard and salt and pepper. Return to the oven and microwave on HIGH for 2½ minutes, stirring after every minute, until thick and smooth. Leave to cool slightly.

3 Beat the egg yolks into the sauce, one at a time. Reserve 15 ml (1 tbsp) cheese and add the rest to the sauce. Stir until well blended.

4 Whisk the egg whites until stiff and fold into the sauce.

5 Spoon the mixture into the buttered dish. Smooth the top and sprinkle with the reserved cheese.

6 Place in the oven and microwave on LOW for 10 minutes until risen. Serve at once.

Serve with a green salad and hot crusty bread and butter.

Cheesy Pie

TIMES PREP.	COOK	METHOD	SETTINGS	SERVINGS
30	22	MICRO. / CONVEN.	HIGH	4

900 g (2 lb) potatoes, peeled
25 g (1 oz) butter or margarine, softened
pinch of grated nutmeg
salt and pepper
200 g (7 oz) mozzarella cheese, thinly sliced
225 g (8 oz) salami, thinly sliced
50 g (2 oz) fresh breadcrumbs
50 g (2 oz) Parmesan cheese, grated

1 Cut the potatoes into very thin slices and arrange one-third in the base of a deep gratin dish. Spread with half the butter or margarine, sprinkle with a little nutmeg and season to taste with salt and pepper.

2 Arrange half the mozzarella cheese and half the salami on top. Cover with half the remaining potato and spread with the remaining butter or margarine. Add a little nutmeg and season to taste with salt and pepper. Top with the remaining mozzarella cheese and salami and neatly arrange the remaining potato slices on top. Cover and microwave on HIGH for 15–20 minutes or until the potato is cooked.

3 Mix the breadcrumbs and Parmesan cheese together and spread evenly over the top. Grill under a preheated grill until golden brown.

Serve hot with a green salad.

Vegetable and Cheese Terrine

TIMES PREP	COOK	METHOD	SETTINGS	SERVINGS
20	15	MICRO.	MEDIUM HIGH	8

100 g (4 oz) carrots, peeled and cut into matchsticks

100 g (4 oz) French beans, trimmed

10 large fresh spinach leaves

500 g (1 lb) full-fat soft cheese

3 egg yolks

15 ml (1 tbsp) lemon juice

salt and pepper

100 g (4 oz) green peppercorns

1 Place the carrots and beans in separate roasting bags. Add 45 ml (3 tbsp) water to each and pierce the bags. Microwave on HIGH for 3 minutes or until just tender, then drain and set aside.

2 Wash the spinach in several changes of water, drain well and place in a bowl. Cover and microwave on HIGH for 1 minute. Drain and rinse under cold running water.

3 Mix the cheese, egg yolks and lemon juice together and season with salt and pepper.

4 Line a 20.5 cm (8 inch) microwave loaf dish with half the spinach leaves. Spread one-quarter of the cheese mixture in the base of the dish and cover with the carrots. Top with one-third of the remaining cheese and arrange the beans on top. Spread over half the remaining cheese and top with the green peppercorns. Finish with the rest of the cheese and cover with the reserved spinach leaves.

5 Cover with cling flim and microwave on MEDIUM for 5 minutes. Give the dish a half turn, then microwave on HIGH for 3–4 minutes or until set. Leave to cool in the pan, then chill before serving.

Serve with fresh tomato sauce (page 114).

Mushroom Cocottes

TIMES PREP	COOK	METHOD	SETTINGS	SERVINGS
8	7	MICRO.	HIGH	4

25 g (1 oz) butter or margarine

100 g (4 oz) button mushrooms, wiped and sliced

2.5 ml (½ level tsp) cornflour

salt and pepper

4 eggs

60 ml (4 tbsp) double cream

50 g (2 oz) Gruyére cheese, thinly sliced

1 Place the butter or margarine in a medium bowl and microwave on HIGH for 45 seconds or until melted. Stir in the mushrooms and microwave on HIGH for 2 minutes.

2 Blend the cornflour with about 5 ml (1 tsp) water. Add to the bowl of mushrooms and microwave on HIGH for 1 minute. Season to taste with salt and pepper.

3 Spoon the mixture into four ramekin dishes and break an egg into each dish. Gently prick each egg yolk. Spoon over the cream and top with the cheese. Microwave on HIGH for 4 minutes or until the eggs are just set.

Serve as a first course with hot buttered toast.

Variation
Use 2 medium onions, skinned and finely chopped, instead of the mushrooms. Microwave for 5–7 minutes in stage 1.

COOK'S TIP

It is necessary to prick egg yolks before microwaving to break the surrounding membrane, which prevents the yolk bursting during cooking. Use a cocktail stick, skewer or a fork.

Minted Brussels and carrots
(Vegetables) *opposite*

MIN

1 0:

1 LOW
2 WARM
3 DEFROST
4 SIMMER
5 MEDIUM
6
7
8
9

DEFROST
  CHICKEN PORTIONS
  PORK CHOPS (4)
  STEAK
  SAUSAGES
  MINCE
  TROUT
REHEAT
  COFFEE
  SOUP
  CASSEROLE
  VEGETABLES
  MEAT PIE
  PLATED MEAL
COOK
  CHICKEN PORTIONS
  ROOT VEGETABLES
  PEAS
  TROUT
  BACON
  CAKE MIX

COOK

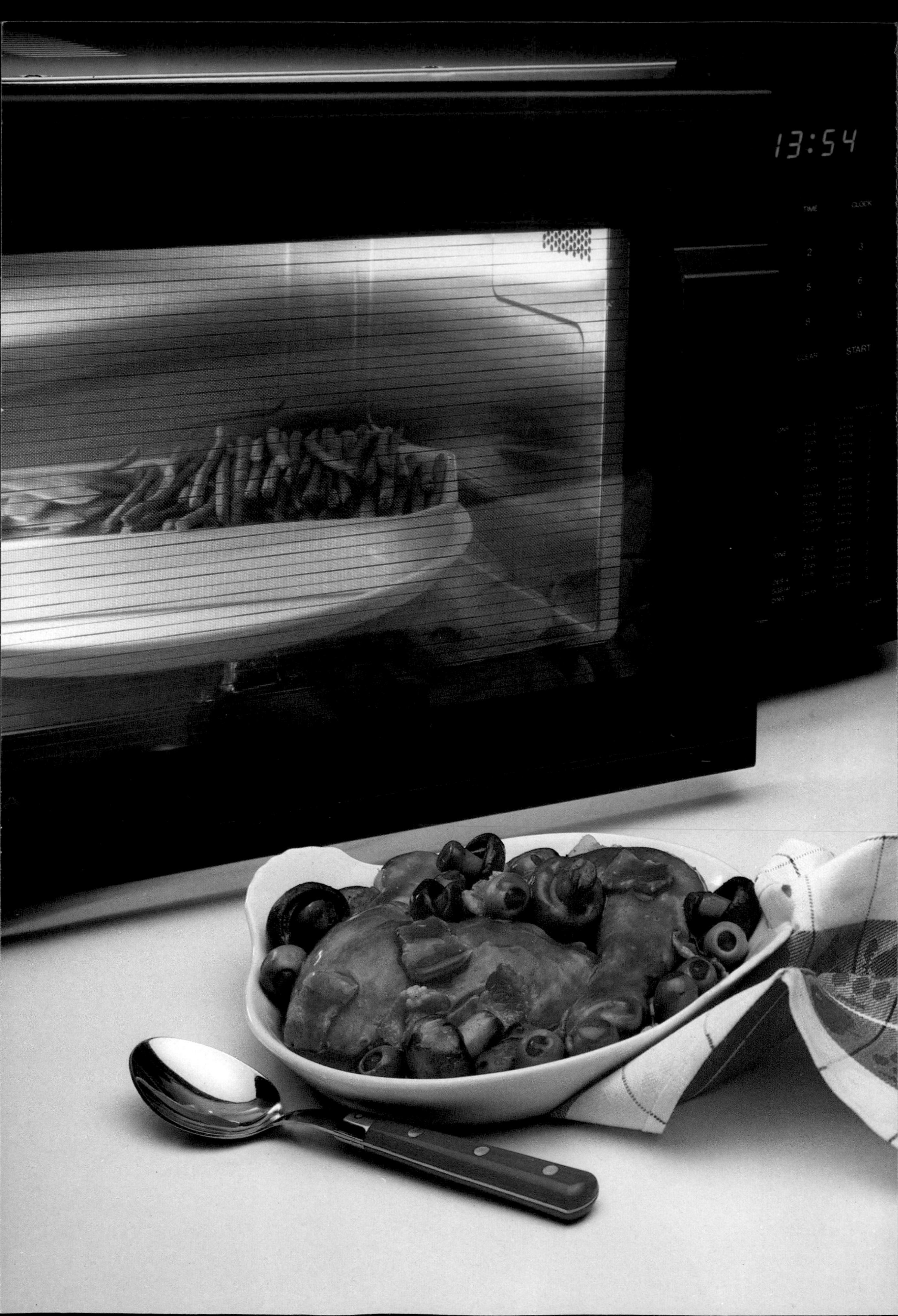
13:54
TIME
CLOCK
START

Pancakes

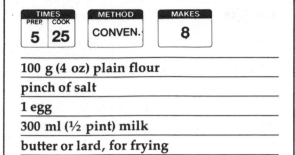

TIMES		METHOD	MAKES
PREP.	COOK	CONVEN.	8
5	25		

---

100 g (4 oz) plain flour

pinch of salt

1 egg

300 ml (½ pint) milk

butter or lard, for frying

---

1 Place the flour and salt in a medium bowl. Make a well in the centre and add the egg. Beat well with a wooden spoon and gradually beat in the milk.

2 Gently heat an 18 cm (7 inch) heavy-based frying pan. Add about 15 oz (½ oz) butter or lard and continue heating until melted, running it around the base and sides of the pan. Pour off any excess fat.

3 Spoon in just enough batter to thinly coat the base of the pan. Fry until golden brown underneath, then turn the pancake over and cook the other side. Transfer to a plate. Repeat with the remaining batter to make a total of 8 pancakes. Stack the pancakes on top of each other.

COOK'S TIP

To reheat pancakes, wrap them in a clean tea towel and microwave on HIGH for 2 minutes or until warmed through.

Spinach and Stilton pancakes

TIMES		METHOD	SETTINGS	SERVINGS
PREP.	COOK	MICRO.	HIGH	4
20	28	CONVEN.		

---

8 pancakes (see left)

For the filling:

900 g (2 lb) fresh spinach

50 g (2 oz) butter or margarine

50 g (2 oz) pine nuts

2.5 ml (½ level tsp) paprika

pinch of grated nutmeg

45 ml (3 level tbsp) plain flour

142 g (5 oz) natural yogurt

salt and pepper

300 ml (½ pint) milk

100 g (4 oz) Stilton cheese, crumbled

---

1 To make the filling, tear the stalks off the spinach and wash the leaves thoroughly. Place in a large bowl, cover and microwave on HIGH for 5 minutes or until soft. Drain and chop.

2 In the same bowl, microwave 25 g (1 oz) butter or margarine on HIGH for 45 seconds or until melted. Add the pine nuts, paprika, nutmeg, 15 ml (1 level tbsp) flour, yogurt and spinach. Season to taste. Microwave on HIGH for 4 minutes or until boiling, then microwave on HIGH for a further 2 minutes, stirring once.

3 Divide the filling between the pancakes, roll up and place in a shallow flameproof dish, seam side down.

4 Place the remaining butter or margarine in a medium bowl and microwave on HIGH for 45 seconds or until melted. Stir in the remaining flour and microwave on HIGH for 30 seconds. Gradually whisk in the milk and microwave on HIGH for 5–7 minutes or until smooth and thick.

5 Stir in the cheese and season to taste. Pour the sauce over the pancakes and microwave on HIGH for 5 minutes until heated through. Grill under a hot grill until golden brown.

Serve with a green salad and crusty rolls.

Spanish chicken in red wine (Poultry) *opposite*

Pizza Flan

TIMES PREP.	COOK	METHOD	SETTINGS	SERVINGS
30	17	MICRO.	HIGH	4

20.5 cm (8 inch) flan case (see page 105)

For the filling:

45 ml (3 tbsp) vegetable oil

450 g (1 lb) onions, skinned and thinly sliced

2 garlic cloves, skinned and crushed

1 green pepper, seeded and thinly sliced

397 g (14 oz) can chopped tomatoes, drained

30 ml (2 level tbsp) tomato purée

2.5 ml (½ tsp) mixed herbs

salt and pepper

200 g (7 oz) mozzarella cheese, thinly sliced

50 g (2 oz) can anchovies, drained

8 black olives, stoned

1 Mix the oil, onions, garlic and green pepper together in a large bowl and microwave on HIGH for 5–7 minutes or until soft.

2 Stir in the tomatoes, tomato purée, herbs and seasoning and microwave on HIGH for 5 minutes.

3 Place the flan case on a serving plate and spoon in the filling. Arrange the cheese, anchovies and olives on top. Microwave on HIGH for 5 minutes or until bubbling and the cheese is melted.

Serve with a green salad.

Leek and Macaroni au Gratin

TIMES PREP.	COOK	METHOD	SETTINGS	SERVINGS
30	18	MICRO. CONVEN.	HIGH	4

125 g (4 oz) short-cut macaroni

salt and pepper

50 g (2 oz) butter or margarine

275 g (10 oz) leeks, trimmed, thinly sliced and washed

50 g (2 oz) plain flour

568 ml (1 pint) milk

225 g (8 oz) Cheddar cheese, grated

25 g (1 oz) fresh breadcrumbs

1 Place the macaroni in a medium bowl and pour over 900 ml (1½ pints) boiling water. Season with salt, cover and microwave on HIGH for 5 minutes. Leave to stand, covered.

2 Microwave the butter or margarine in a medium flameproof casserole on HIGH for 45 seconds or until melted. Stir in the leeks and microwave on HIGH for 5 minutes or until soft.

3 Stir in the flour and microwave on HIGH for 30 seconds. Gradually stir in the milk. Microwave on HIGH for 5 minutes or until boiling and thickened, stirring occasionally. Stir in two-thirds of the cheese and season to taste.

4 Drain the pasta, add to the cheese sauce and mix lightly together.

5 Combine the reserved cheese with the breadcrumbs and sprinkle evenly over the dish. Grill under a preheated grill until golden brown.

Serve with a green vegetable such as broccoli.

Rice and Pasta

Rice and dried pasta need the same amount of time in the microwave to rehydrate and cook as they do when cooked in the conventional way. However, there are advantages to using the microwave to cook them.

Pasta

Without any of the intense direct heat underneath the pan, pasta will not stick to the bottom. That said, care must still be taken to ensure that the pasta does not stick together during cooking. Always cook pasta in plenty of boiling salted water. As an extra precaution, add 15 ml (1 tbsp) vegetable oil to every 1.4 litre (2½ pints) water. To save time add boiling water from the kettle to the bowl of pasta.

Cook pasta until it is tender but still firm, or *al dente*. Part of the cooking occurs during the standing time which is essential when cooking dried pasta, otherwise prolonged microwaving will cause the pasta to become soggy or watery. Pasta should be covered and left to stand in its cooking liquid for 5–10 minutes, depending on the type of pasta shape. Make the sauce during standing time. It may be more convenient, depending on how long it takes to make the sauce, to cook the pasta conventionally and use the microwave for making the sauce.

Fresh pasta needs to be cooked for only 1 minute and should be drained and served immediately.

Once pasta is tossed in a sauce it can be reheated quickly if necessary and still retain its freshness. Leftover pasta dishes also reheat superbly, especially if they are mixed with a sauce which helps to retain moisture. Loosely cover the dish and microwave until heated through.

Rice

Rice can be microwaved in the same way that it is cooked conventionally. Cook in plenty of boiling salted water and leave to stand for 10 minutes, then drain. Or use the absorption method and mix the rice in double its volume of cold water and cook until tender but still firm, again allowing for standing. With microwaving, rice grains stay beautifully separate and will not stick to the bottom of the pan.

The amount of time needed for cooking rice depends to a large extent on the type of rice being cooked. Be guided by conventional cooking times but always allow for further cooking during standing.

Risottos, pilafs and paellas can all be very successfully microwaved. Vegetables and sauces can be microwaved in less time than it would take to conventionally cook them and they all reheat without loss of flavour as does plain boiled rice. Loosely cover the dish of rice with cling film or reheat in a pierced roasting bag. Add about 5–10 ml (1–2 tsp) water just to create a little steam during heating.

Green Rice

TIMES PREP	TIMES COOK	METHOD	SETTINGS	SERVINGS
10	27	MICRO.	HIGH	6

75 g (3 oz) butter or margarine

450 g (1 lb) long grain white rice

30 ml (2 tbsp) chopped fresh marjoram

900 ml (1½ pints) boiling chicken stock

225 g (8 oz) fresh broccoli

salt and pepper

25 g (1 oz) flaked almonds, toasted

1 Place 50 g (2 oz) butter or margarine in a large casserole and microwave on HIGH for 1 minute until foaming.

2 Stir in the rice and marjoram. Pour over the boiling stock and stir well. Cover and microwave on HIGH for 13 minutes. Leave to stand, covered, for 10 minutes.

3 Break the broccoli into small florets and place in a roasting bag with the remaining butter or margarine and 30 ml (2 tbsp) water. Fasten the top and pierce the bag with a fork. Microwave on HIGH for 3 minutes. Tip into the rice and mix carefully with a fork. Garnish with the almonds and serve.

Serve with roast chicken or turkey.

COOK'S TIP

Choose the calabrese broccoli which has thicker stems and more florets than the sprouting variety.

To toast almonds, place them on a large plate and microwave on HIGH for 8–10 minutes, stirring frequently until golden brown.

Eastern Pilau Rice

TIMES PREP	TIMES COOK	METHOD	SETTINGS	SERVINGS
10	31	MICRO.	HIGH	4

50 g (2 oz) butter or margarine

2 medium onions, skinned and thinly sliced

4 cloves

5 ml (1 level tsp) cardamom seeds

5 ml (1 level tsp) cinnamon

225 g (8 oz) basmati or other long grain white rice

50 g (2 oz) seedless raisins

salt and pepper

1 Place the butter or margarine in a large casserole and microwave on HIGH for 45 seconds or until melted. Stir in the onion and microwave on HIGH for 5–7 minutes or until soft, stirring once. Add the spices, stir well, and microwave on HIGH for 1 minute.

2 Add the rice and raisins to the casserole and mix well. Pour over 600 ml (1 pint) boiling water, stir once, then cover and microwave on HIGH for 12 minutes. Leave to stand, covered, for 10 minutes.

3 Season to taste, mix lightly with a fork and serve immediately.

Serve as an accompaniment to grilled or roast lamb.

Orange Rice

TIMES PREP. 30 COOK 31	METHOD MICRO.	SETTINGS HIGH	SERVINGS 6

50 g (2 oz) butter or margarine

1 small onion, skinned and finely chopped

3 celery sticks, trimmed and thinly sliced

450 g (1 lb) long grain white rice

finely grated rind and juice of 2 oranges

30 ml (2 tbsp) chopped fresh mint

salt and pepper

100 g (4 oz) Brazil nuts, shredded

1 Place the butter or margarine in a large casserole and microwave on HIGH for 45 seconds or until melted.

2 Stir in the onion and celery and microwave on HIGH for 5–7 minutes or until soft, stirring once. Stir in the rice, orange rind and mint.

3 Make up the orange juice to 600 ml (1 pint) with boiling water and add to the rice. Microwave on HIGH for 5 minutes or until boiling. Stir well, cover and microwave on HIGH for 13 minutes. Leave to stand for 5 minutes.

4 Season to taste and stir in the Brazil nuts with a fork. Serve immediately.

Serve as an accompaniment to grilled poultry or a creamed chicken dish.

Dhal

TIMES PREP. 10 COOK 27	METHOD MICRO.	SETTINGS HIGH	SERVINGS 4

30 ml (2 tbsp) vegetable oil

1 medium onion, skinned and finely chopped

3 garlic cloves, skinned and crushed

1 green chilli, seeded and thinly sliced

100 g (4 oz) red lentils

600 ml (1 pint) boiling chicken stock

5 ml (1 level tsp) salt

1.25 ml (¼ level tsp) turmeric

1.25 ml (¼ level tsp) chilli powder

1.25 ml (¼ level tsp) ground cumin

fresh coriander, to garnish

1 Place the oil, onion, garlic and chilli in a large bowl and microwave on HIGH for 5–7 minutes or until soft, stirring once.

2 Stir in the lentils, stock, salt and spices. Cover and microwave on HIGH for 20 minutes, stirring once.

3 Beat well with a wooden spoon or for a smoother texture, purée in a blender or food processor.

4 Garnish with fresh coriander and serve.

Serve as an accompaniment to chicken or lamb curry.

COOK'S TIP

For a thicker, drier dhal, microwave on HIGH, uncovered, for a further 3 minutes after puréeing.

Chicken Risotto

TIMES		METHOD	SETTINGS	SERVINGS
PREP. **40**	COOK **30**	MICRO.	· HIGH	4

30 ml (2 tbsp) vegetable oil

1 large onion, skinned and chopped

1 leek, sliced and washed

1 green pepper, seeded and sliced

2.5 ml (½ level tsp) cayenne

5 ml (1 level tsp) ground cumin

350 g (12 oz) cooked chicken, diced

finely grated rind and juice of 1 lemon

25 g (1 oz) stoned black or green olives

900 ml (1½ pints) boiling chicken stock

450 g (1 lb) long grain white rice

salt and pepper

chopped fresh parsley, to garnish

1 Place the oil, onion, vegetables and spices in a large casserole dish and microwave on HIGH for 5–7 minutes or until soft, stirring once.

2 Stir in the chicken, lemon rind and juice, olives, stock, rice and seasoning. Mix well, cover and microwave on HIGH for 13 minutes. Leave to stand, covered, for 10 minutes.

3 Mix lightly with a fork and serve hot, garnished with chopped parsley.

Serve as a main dish with a green salad.

COOK'S TIP

For a more substantial dish, top the risotto with 175 g (6 oz) grated Cheddar cheese and place under a hot grill until melted and golden.

Country-Style Risotto

TIMES		METHOD	SETTINGS	SERVINGS
PREP. **20**	COOK **20**	MICRO.	HIGH	4

45 ml (3 tbsp) vegetable oil

2 medium onions, skinned and chopped

2 celery sticks, trimmed and thinly sliced

100 g (4 oz) courgettes, sliced

100 g (4 oz) shelled broad beans

350 g (12 oz) Italian arborio or long grain white rice

600 ml (1 pint) boiling chicken stock

salt and pepper

100 g (4 oz) garlic sausage, thinly sliced

45 ml (3 tbsp) chopped fresh parsley

25 g (1 oz) freshly grated Parmesan cheese

1 Place the oil, onion and celery in a large bowl and microwave on HIGH for 5–7 minutes or until soft, stirring once.

2 Stir in the courgettes, beans, rice and stock. Cover and microwave on HIGH for 13 minutes. Leave to stand, covered, for 10 minutes.

3 Carefully toss with a fork, season to taste and mix in the sausage, parsley and Parmesan cheese. Serve immediately.

Serve with hot garlic bread and a green salad.

Spaghetti with Mussels

TIMES		METHOD	SETTINGS	SERVINGS
PREP.	COOK			
15	19	MICRO.	HIGH	4

75 ml (5 tbsp) vegetable oil

1 garlic clove, skinned and crushed

60 ml (4 tbsp) chopped fresh parsley

397 g (14 oz) can tomatoes

15 ml (1 tbsp) red wine vinegar

salt and pepper

400 g (14 oz) spaghetti

450 g (1 lb) frozen shelled mussels, thawed

1 Mix 45 ml (3 tbsp) oil, the garlic and 30 ml (2 tbsp) parsley together in a medium bowl and microwave on HIGH for about 2 minutes or until the garlic is soft.

2 Place the tomatoes and vinegar in a food processor or blender and purée until smooth. Add to the garlic and parsley and season to taste. Microwave on HIGH for 5 minutes.

3 Place the pasta in a 2.6 litre (4½ pint) bowl. Pour over 1.7 litres (3 pints) boiling water, add salt to taste, cover and microwave on HIGH for 7 minutes. Leave to stand, covered.

4 Rinse the mussels, removing any broken shell and add to the sauce. Microwave on HIGH for 5 minutes, stirring once. Check that the mussels are heated through.

5 Drain the pasta, tip into a heated serving bowl and toss with the remaining oil. Pour over the sauce and serve immediately, sprinkled with the reserved parsley.

Serve with hot garlic bread and a crisp green salad.

COOK'S TIP

Use three 142 g (5 oz) jars of mussels in brine, drained, instead of frozen mussels.

Tagliatelle with Smoked Ham and Peas

TIMES		METHOD	SETTINGS	SERVINGS
PREP.	COOK			
25	17	MICRO.	HIGH	4

225 g (8 oz) dried tagliatelle

salt and pepper

1 medium onion, skinned and thinly sliced

30 ml (2 tbsp) vegetable oil

100 g (4 oz) fresh shelled or frozen peas

225 g (8 oz) piece smoked ham

150 ml (5 fl oz) double cream

50 g (2 oz) freshly grated Parmesan cheese

1 Place the tagliatelle in a 2.6 litre (4½ pint) bowl and pour over 1.7 litres (3 pints) boiling water. Add salt to taste and stir once. Cover and microwave on HIGH for 7 minutes. Leave to stand, covered.

2 Mix the onion and oil together in a medium bowl and microwave on HIGH for 2 minutes. Stir in the peas, cover and microwave on HIGH for 5 minutes or until the onion and peas are tender.

3 Meanwhile, cut the ham into matchstick pieces. Add to the onion and peas along with the cream. Season to taste with salt and pepper and microwave on HIGH for 3 minutes or until hot, stirring once or twice.

4 Drain the noodles and tip into a warmed serving dish. Pour over the sauce and toss lightly. Sprinkle with the cheese and serve.

Serve with a mixed salad.

Paprika Pasta

TIMES PREP. | COOK 10 | 17	METHOD MICRO.	SETTINGS HIGH	SERVINGS 4

225 g (8 oz) pasta shapes, such as twirls

salt and pepper

75 g (3 oz) butter or margarine

2 medium onions, skinned and thinly sliced

142 ml (5 fl oz) soured cream

15 ml (1 level tbsp) paprika

1 Place the pasta in a 2.6 litre (4½ pint) bowl and pour over 1.4 litres (2½ pints) boiling water. Add salt to taste, stir, cover and microwave on HIGH for 7 minutes. Leave to stand, covered.

2 Place the butter or margarine in a medium bowl and microwave on HIGH for 45 seconds or until melted. Stir in the onions and microwave on HIGH for 5–7 minutes, or until soft, stirring once.

3 Stir in the soured cream and paprika. Season to taste with salt and pepper.

4 Drain the pasta and return to the bowl. Pour over the onion and soured cream mixture and toss lightly together. Microwave on HIGH for 1–2 minutes until heated through.

Serve as an accompaniment to grilled or roast meats.

Tuna and Tomato Pasta

TIMES PREP. | COOK 15 | 23	METHOD MICRO. CONVEN.	SETTINGS HIGH	SERVINGS 4

225 g (8 oz) pasta shapes, such as bows

salt and pepper

45 ml (3 tbsp) vegetable oil

2 medium onions, skinned and sliced

1 garlic clove, skinned and crushed

397 g (14 oz) can tomatoes, drained and chopped

198 g (7 oz) can tuna, drained and flaked

45 ml (3 tbsp) chopped fresh parsley

142 ml (5 fl oz) soured cream

For the topping:

50 g (2 oz) can anchovies

75 g (3 oz) fresh bread

25 g (1 oz) butter or margarine

1 Place the pasta and salt to taste in a 2.6 litre (4½ pint) bowl. Pour over 1.4 litres (2½ pints) boiling water. Stir once, cover and microwave on HIGH for 7 minutes. Leave to stand, covered.

2 Mix the oil, onion and garlic together in a medium bowl and microwave on HIGH for 5–7 minutes, or until soft.

3 Stir in the tomatoes and tuna and microwave on HIGH for 3 minutes until bubbling. Add the parsley and season with pepper.

4 Drain the pasta and return to the bowl. Pour over the tomato sauce and toss lightly together. Set aside.

5 Drain the anchovy oil into a frying pan and place the bread and anchovies in a food processor or blender. Mix well.

6 Heat the butter with the anchovy oil, add the anchovy crumbs and stir over a high heat until crisp.

7 Spoon the soured cream over the pasta and gently mix in. Microwave on HIGH for 1 minute to heat through. Sprinkle with the anchovy crumbs and serve.

Serve with a green salad.

Spaghetti Carbonara

TIMES PREP.	TIMES COOK	METHOD	SETTINGS	SERVINGS
15	14	MICRO.	HIGH	4

225 g (8 oz) spaghetti

salt and pepper

2 eggs

100 g (4 oz) Cheddar cheese, finely grated

45 ml (3 level tbsp) freshly grated Parmesan cheese

225 g (8 oz) streaky bacon, rinded and chopped

150 ml (5 fl oz) double cream

chopped fresh parsley, to garnish

grated Parmesan cheese, to serve

1 Place the spaghetti in a 2.6 litre (4½ pint) bowl, pour over 1.4 litres (2½ pints) boiling water. Add salt to taste, and stir once. Cover and microwave on HIGH for 7 minutes. Leave to stand, covered.

2 Beat together the eggs and cheeses.

3 Place the bacon in a medium bowl, cover with absorbent kitchen paper, and microwave on HIGH for 5 minutes.

4 Stir in the cream and season to taste. Microwave on HIGH for 2 minutes or until heated through.

5 Drain the pasta and tip into a warmed serving dish. Pour over the egg and cheese mixture and mix well. Add the bacon and cream mixture. Mix well and sprinkle with parsley. Serve at once with Parmesan cheese.

Serve with French bread and a green salad.

Ham and Mushroom Bake

TIMES PREP.	TIMES COOK	METHOD	SETTINGS	SERVINGS
30	30	MICRO. CONVEN.	HIGH	4

225 g (8 oz) pasta shapes, such as twirls, small shells or quills

salt and pepper

30 ml (2 tbsp) vegetable oil

2 medium onions, skinned and chopped

2 garlic cloves, skinned and crushed

225 g (8 oz) ham, diced

100 g (4 oz) button mushrooms, wiped

1 red pepper, seeded and chopped

30 ml (2 level tbsp) plain flour

30 ml (2 level tbsp) tomato purée

15 ml (1 level tbsp) dried oregano

397 g (14 oz) can chopped tomatoes

100 g (4 oz) Cheddar cheese, grated

1 Place the pasta in a 2.6 litre (4½ pint) bowl and add 1.4 litres (2½ pints) boiling water. Add salt to taste and stir once. Cover and microwave on HIGH for 7 minutes. Leave to stand, covered.

2 Mix the oil, onion and garlic together in a large flameproof casserole and microwave on HIGH for 5–7 minutes, or until soft, stirring once.

3 Stir in the ham, mushrooms, red pepper, flour, tomato purée, oregano and tomatoes with their juice and season to taste with salt and pepper. Pour over 300 ml (½ pint) boiling water. Microwave on HIGH for 8 minutes, stirring once or twice.

4 Drain the pasta and stir into the sauce. Microwave on HIGH for 5 minutes.

5 Sprinkle with the cheese and brown under a hot grill.

Serve with a green vegetable or salad to make a complete meal.

Fish

The moist delicate texture of fish is especially suitable for microwave cooking. Fish cooks in minutes and its natural fresh flavour is enhanced by cooking in the microwave oven.

To help keep fish moist during microwaving, brush the fish with oil or melted butter and cover tightly. Slit the skin of whole fish to prevent it from bursting. Very large fish may need to be curled in a round dish to fit in the microwave oven. Two fish can be microwaved in separate dishes, one on top of the other at right angles. Reposition the dishes top to bottom halfway through cooking. It may be necessary to shield the tail ends of whole fish, otherwise they may overcook.

Place the thinner ends of fish fillets towards the centre of the dish and if cooking more than two fillets overlap the thin ends, separating them with cling film.

Always slightly undercook fish as it will continue to cook during standing. Remember, too, that fish should be undercooked if you intend to reheat it later. Fish is cooked when the flesh flakes easily when tested with a fork.

Making fish casseroles and other fish dishes is much simpler when using the microwave. Fish can be poached in water, stock or court bouillon which can be strained and used for making the sauce. A fish dish can also be assembled and then heated through in the microwave without altering flavour. The casserole can be topped with breadcrumbs or cheese and finished off under the grill.

Fish cannot be deep-fried in the microwave and breadcrumb-coated fish, including fish fingers, will not become crisp. However, breadcrumbed fish can be cooked in the microwave and then crisped under the grill – a way of 'frying' fish which should appeal to slimmers.

Fish starters can be prepared in advance and reheated in the microwave. Or use the microwave to cook the fish for making mousses and jellied moulds.

Paupiettes of Sole

TIMES		METHOD	SETTINGS	SERVINGS
PREP	COOK	MICRO.	HIGH	6
30	14			

220 g (8 oz) can pink salmon

1 egg white

25 g (1 oz) fresh breadcrumbs

1 bunch of watercress, washed and trimmed

salt and pepper

6 sole or plaice fillets, skinned

50 ml (2 fl oz) dry white wine

50 ml (2 fl oz) double cream

1 To make the stuffing, drain the salmon, reserving the juice, and remove the skin and bones. Put into a blender or food processor along with the egg white, breadcrumbs and half the bunch of watercress. Season to taste and mix until very smooth.

2 Cut the fish fillets in half lengthways. Season to taste and spread with the stuffing mixture. Roll up each fillet and secure with wooden cocktail sticks.

3 Stand the fish roll-ups on their ends in a flan dish, packing them close together. Make up the salmon juice to 75 ml (3 fl oz) with water and add the wine. Pour the liquid over the fish. Cover and microwave on HIGH for 6 minutes or until tender, turning the dish once.

4 Using a slotted spoon, transfer the roll-ups to a heated serving dish and keep hot.

5 Add the cream to the pan juices and microwave on HIGH for 3 minutes or until boiling, stirring occasionally, then continue microwaving for another 3–5 minutes until the sauce has reduced and is thickened. Season to taste and pour the sauce over the fish. Garnish with the remaining watercress and serve at once.

Serve with boiled new potatoes and a green salad.

Salmon Steaks Parmesan

TIMES		METHOD	SETTINGS	SERVINGS
PREP	COOK	MICRO.	HIGH	4
15	20			

50 g (2 oz) butter or margarine

1 medium onion, skinned and finely chopped

4 salmon steaks, each about 4 cm (1½ inches) thick and weighing about 175 g (6 oz)

150 ml (5 fl oz) double cream

30 ml (2 level tbsp) French mustard

salt and pepper

50 g (2 oz) fresh breadcrumbs

45 ml (3 level tbsp) freshly grated Parmesan cheese

1 Place half the butter or margarine in a shallow dish and microwave on HIGH for 45 seconds or until melted. Add the onion and microwave on HIGH for 5–7 minutes or until soft, stirring once.

2 Arrange the salmon steaks in a single layer on top of the onions, with the thinnest parts towards the centre.

3 Blend the cream, mustard and seasoning together and spoon it over the fish. Cover and microwave on HIGH for 8 minutes or until the fish is tender, turning the dish once.

4 Place the remaining butter or margarine in a small bowl and microwave on HIGH for 45 seconds or until melted. Stir in the breadcrumbs and cheese.

5 Spoon the crumb mixture over the fish and grill under a hot grill until golden brown. Serve at once.

Serve this luxurious dish with boiled new potatoes and a green vegetable.

Haddock Mousse

TIMES		METHOD	SETTINGS	SERVINGS
PREP. 20	COOK 7	MICRO.	HIGH	4

450 g (1 lb) haddock fillets

15 ml (1 level tbsp) powdered gelatine

50 ml (2 fl oz) white wine vinegar

4 hard-boiled eggs

450 ml (¾ pint) mayonnaise

10 ml (2 level tsp) tomato purée

5 ml (1 tsp) anchovy essence

salt and pepper

2 egg whites

1 small bunch of watercress, washed and trimmed

sprig of fresh dill, to garnish

1 Arrange the fish in a single layer in a shallow dish. Cover and microwave on HIGH for 6 minutes or until tender. Flake the fish, discarding skin and bones.

2 Sprinkle the gelatine over the vinegar in a small bowl. Leave to soften slightly then add 225 ml (8 fl oz) hot water. Microwave on HIGH for 30 seconds or until dissolved.

3 Place the hard-boiled eggs, 150 ml (¼ pint) mayonnaise, tomato purée, anchovy essence, seasoning and fish in a blender or food processor and mix until smooth. Gradually stir in the gelatine. Tip into a bowl and refrigerate just until the mixture is thick enough to coat the back of a spoon.

6 Whisk the egg whites until stiff and fold into the fish mixture. Spoon into a 1.7–2.3 litre (3–4 pint) ring mould and refrigerate for about 2 hours until set.

7 Finely chop the watercress and beat into the remaining mayonnaise.

8 Unmould the mousse on to a serving plate. Spoon over a little of the green mayonnaise and garnish with the sprig of dill. Serve the remaining mayonnaise separately.

Serve as a main course with wholemeal rolls and a green salad.

Haddock au Gratin

TIMES		METHOD	SETTINGS	SERVINGS
PREP. 30	COOK 17	MICRO. CONVEN.	HIGH	4

450 g (1 lb) haddock fillet

225 g (8 oz) smoked haddock fillet

60 ml (4 tbsp) dry white wine

6 black peppercorns

1 bay leaf

1 small onion, skinned and thinly sliced

50 g (2 oz) butter or margarine

100 g (4 oz) button mushrooms, wiped and sliced

45 ml (3 level tbsp) plain flour

pepper

75 g (3 oz) Cheddar cheese, finely grated

25 g (1 oz) fresh breadcrumbs

25 g (1 oz) walnuts, finely chopped

1 Place the fish in a shallow dish. Pour over the wine and 300 ml (½ pint) water. Add the peppercorns, bay leaf and onion. Cover and microwave on HIGH for 5 minutes, turning the dish once.

2 Strain off the liquid and reserve. Flake the fish and discard the peppercorns, bay leaf and onion.

3 Place the butter or margarine in a medium flameproof casserole and microwave on HIGH for 45 seconds or until melted. Stir in the mushrooms and microwave on HIGH for 1 minute. Blend in the flour and microwave on HIGH for 30 seconds. Gradually stir in the cooking liquid and microwave on HIGH for 5–6 minutes, stirring after every minute, until boiling.

4 Season to taste with pepper and stir in half the cheese and the fish. Microwave on HIGH for 2 minutes.

5 Mix the breadcrumbs, remaining cheese and walnuts together. Spoon the mixture over the fish and brown under a hot grill.

Serve with mashed potatoes and spinach.

Stuffed Trout with Caper Sauce

TIMES		METHOD	SETTINGS	SERVINGS
PREP	COOK			
30	21	MICRO.	HIGH	4

150 g (5 oz) butter or margarine

1 small onion, skinned and finely chopped

50 g (2 oz) mushrooms, wiped and finely chopped

45 ml (3 tbsp) lemon juice

half a small fennel bulb, finely chopped

50 g (2 oz) fresh brown breadcrumbs

1 egg white, lightly beaten

salt and pepper

4 trout, each weighing 175 g (6 oz), cleaned and heads removed

3 egg yolks

15 ml (1 level tbsp) capers

1 Place 50 g (2 oz) butter or margarine in a medium bowl and microwave on HIGH for 45 seconds or until melted. Stir in the onion, mushrooms, lemon juice and 15 ml (1 tbsp) chopped fennel. Cover and microwave on HIGH for 5–7 minutes or until soft, stirring once. Stir in the breadcrumbs and egg white and season.

2 Stuff each trout with some of the mixture. Arrange the fish in a shallow oblong dish, head next to tail and stuffing pockets uppermost.

3 Cover and microwave on HIGH for 5 minutes. Reposition the fish, cover and microwave for a further 5 minutes or until tender. Leave to stand, covered.

5 Melt the remaining butter or margarine in a medium bowl on HIGH.

6 Whisk together the egg yolks and remaining lemon juice and season to taste. Gradually whisk into the butter or margarine. Microwave on HIGH for 45 seconds, whisking every 15 seconds, until thick enough to coat the back of a spoon. Remove from the microwave and whisk for a further 20 seconds to cool slightly. Stir in the capers and serve with the trout.

Serve with potatoes and a green vegetable.

Poached Trout with Horseradish Cream

TIMES		METHOD	SETTINGS	SERVINGS
PREP	COOK			
15	6	MICRO.	HIGH	3

3 trout, each weighing 225 g (8 oz), cleaned and heads removed

45 ml (3 tbsp) cider vinegar

30 ml (2 level tbsp) natural yogurt

60 ml (4 level tbsp) mayonnaise

30 ml (2 level tbsp) horseradish sauce

salt and pepper

curly endive or lettuce and cucumber, to garnish

1 In an oblong dish, arrange the trout with their backbones to the outside. Pour over the vinegar and 50 ml (2 fl oz) water. Cover and microwave on HIGH for 3 minutes. Turn the fish over and reposition it. Cover and microwave on HIGH for 3 minutes. Leave to stand until cold.

2 When cold, drain the fish, cut in half along the backbones and remove the skin and bones. Arrange on a flat serving dish and keep cool.

3 Mix the yogurt, mayonnaise and horseradish sauce together and season to taste. Pour the sauce over the fish. Garnish with the endive or lettuce and cucumber and serve.

Serve with thinly sliced brown bread and butter.

COOK'S TIP

When buying trout make sure that the fish are firm and have a slimy skin and bright eyes.

Paella

TIMES		METHOD	SETTINGS	SERVINGS
PREP.	COOK	MICRO.	HIGH	6
15	53	CONVEN.		

1 small onion, skinned and finely chopped

2 garlic cloves, skinned and crushed

15 ml (1 tbsp) vegetable oil

350 g (12 oz) long grain rice

900 ml (1½ pints) boiling chicken stock

few saffron strands

salt and pepper

6 chicken thighs

100 g (4 oz) frozen peas

1 red pepper, seeded and sliced

100 g (4 oz) unpeeled prawns

225 g (8 oz) frozen mussels, thawed

1 Mix the onion, garlic and oil together in a large serving bowl, and microwave on HIGH for 5–7 minutes or until soft, stirring once.

2 Stir in the rice, stock and saffron. Season to taste with salt and pepper. Cover and microwave on HIGH for 13 minutes, stirring once. Leave to stand, covered.

3 Place the chicken on a plate and microwave on HIGH for 5 minutes. Turn the chicken pieces over and microwave on HIGH for a further 5 minutes or until tender. Grill under a hot grill until golden brown. Alternatively, heat a browning dish according to manufacturer's instructions, brown the chicken, then microwave for 10 minutes, turning the chicken over once.

4 Place the peas and pepper in a bowl and microwave on HIGH for 3 minutes. Stir in the prawns and mussels, cover and microwave on HIGH for 5 minutes.

5 Lightly stir the rice with a fork and mix with the mussels, prawns and vegetables. Arrange the chicken on top. Cover and microwave on HIGH for 5 minutes or until heated through.

Serve with a green salad and French bread.

Curried Cod Steaks

TIMES		METHOD	SETTINGS	SERVINGS
PREP.	COOK	MICRO.	HIGH	4
8	21			

50 g (2 oz) butter or margarine

1 large onion, skinned and sliced

5 ml (1 level tsp) ground coriander

5 ml (1 level tsp) ground cumin

5 ml (1 level tsp) turmeric

4 cod steaks, each weighing 175 g (6 oz)

142 g (5 oz) natural yogurt

salt and pepper

chopped fresh parsley, to garnish

1 Place the butter or margarine in a shallow dish and microwave on HIGH for 1 minute or until melted. Add the onion, stir well and microwave on HIGH for 5–7 minutes or until soft. Stir in the spices and microwave on HIGH for 2 minutes, stirring once.

2 Arrange the fish on top of the onion and spices. Cover and microwave on HIGH for 5 minutes. Turn the fish over and microwave on HIGH for a further 5 minutes or until the fish flakes when tested with a fork.

3 Remove the fish with a slotted spoon and arrange in a warmed serving dish. Keep hot.

4 Stir the yogurt into the pan juices and season to taste with salt and pepper. Microwave on HIGH for 1 minute or until heated through.

5 Pour the sauce over the fish and sprinkle with chopped parsley. Serve at once.

Serve with rice and a green vegetable.

Scallops in Cream Sauce

TIMES		METHOD	SETTINGS	SERVINGS
PREP.	COOK	MICRO.	HIGH	4
25	35	CONVEN.		

700 g (1½ lb) potatoes, peeled and cut into small pieces

salt and pepper

1 egg, beaten

450 g (1 lb) frozen scallops, thawed

225 g (8 oz) button mushrooms, wiped and sliced

150 ml (¼ pint) dry cider

15 ml (1 tbsp) lemon juice

25 g (1 oz) butter or margarine

25 g (1 oz) plain flour

150 ml (5 fl oz) double cream

chopped fresh parsley, to garnish

1 Cook the potatoes in boiling salted water in the conventional way. Drain and mash with the egg and seasoning.

2 Meanwhile, slice each scallop in half and place in a medium casserole together with the mushrooms, cider, lemon juice and 150 ml (¼ pint) water. Cover and microwave on HIGH for 10 minutes, stirring once. Strain, reserving 300 ml (½ pint) cooking liquid.

3 Place the butter or margarine in a medium bowl and microwave on HIGH for 45 seconds or until melted. Stir in the flour and microwave on HIGH for 30 seconds. Gradually whisk in the reserved cooking liquid and the cream. Microwave on HIGH for 3 minutes or until thickened, whisking frequently. Season to taste.

4 Stir the scallops and mushrooms into the sauce. Spoon into four individual gratin dishes or scallop shells.

5 Spoon the potatoes into a large piping bag fitted with a large star nozzle and pipe around the borders of the dishes. Microwave on HIGH for 5 minutes until heated through.

6 Grill under a hot grill until golden brown. Garnish with parsley and serve.

Serve with a mixed green salad.

Peppered Mackerel Flan

TIMES		METHOD	SETTINGS	SERVINGS
PREP.	COOK	MICRO.	LOW	6
25	10			

23cm (9 in) flan case (see page 105)

For the filling:

2 smoked mackerel fillets with crushed peppercorns, each weighing 100 g (4 oz)

3 eggs

15 ml (1 level tbsp) horseradish sauce

284 ml (10 fl oz) soured cream

salt and pepper

paprika, to garnish

1 Remove the skin from the mackerel fillets and coarsely flake the flesh, discarding the bones.

2 Beat together the eggs, horseradish sauce and soured cream. Season to taste with salt and pepper and fold in the fish.

3 Spoon the mixture into the flan case and microwave on LOW for 6 minutes or until just set – the centre should still quiver slightly. Give the dish a quarter turn three times during cooking. Leave to cool. Serve warm, sprinkled with paprika.

Serve with a mixed salad.

Sweet and Sour Fish Casserole

TIMES PREP / COOK	METHOD	SETTINGS	SERVINGS
10 / 24	MICRO.	HIGH	4

75 g (3 oz) soft brown sugar

75 ml (5 tbsp) cider vinegar

45 ml (3 tbsp) soy sauce

45 ml (3 level tbsp) cornflour

1 green pepper, seeded and thinly sliced

237 g (8 oz) can crushed pineapple

397 g (14 oz) can tomatoes

450 g (1 lb) firm white fish, such as cod or haddock

225 g (8 oz) peeled prawns

1 In a large casserole, blend the sugar, vinegar, soy sauce and cornflour together. Microwave on HIGH for 3 minutes or until just boiling, stirring once.

2 Stir in the green pepper and the canned pineapple and tomatoes with juices. Cover and microwave on HIGH for 5 minutes until boiling, the continue microwaving on HIGH for 10 minutes.

3 Meanwhile, cut the fish into 5 cm (2 inch) pieces.

4 Stir the fish into the sauce. Cover and microwave on HIGH for 6 minutes or until the fish is tender. Stir in the prawns, cover and microwave on HIGH for about 1 minute just to heat through. Serve at once.

Serve with rice.

Kedgeree

TIMES PREP / COOK	METHOD	SETTINGS	SERVINGS
25 / 31	MICRO.	HIGH	4

225 g (8 oz) long grain rice

450 g (1 lb) smoked haddock fillet

50 g (2 oz) butter or margarine, cut into small pieces

1 large onion, skinned and chopped

10 ml (2 level tsp) curry powder

5 ml (1 level tsp) grated nutmeg

1 bunch of watercress, washed and trimmed

30 ml (2 tbsp) single cream

salt and pepper

2 hard-boiled eggs

1 Place the rice and 600 ml (1 pint) boiling water in a large casserole. Stir once, then cover and microwave on HIGH for 12 minutes. Leave to stand, covered.

2 Place the haddock in a large dish, cover and microwave on HIGH for 6 minutes, turning the dish once. Remove the skin and flake the fish, discarding any bones. Stir the fish into the rice.

3 Place the butter or margarine in a medium bowl and microwave on HIGH for 45 seconds or until melted. Stir in the onion, curry powder and nutmeg. Cover and microwave on HIGH for 5–7 minutes or until the onion is soft, stirring once. Stir it into the rice.

4 Finely chop half the watercress and stir into the rice mixture along with the cream. Season to taste with pepper and add salt only if necessary. Cover and microwave on HIGH for 5 minutes to heat through.

5 Cut each egg into quarters and arrange on the kedgeree. Garnish with the remaining watercress and serve the dish immediately.

Serve with a crispy salad made with apples, nuts and celery.

Peking-duck (Poultry) *opposite*

Monkfish in White Wine

TIMES		METHOD	SETTINGS	SERVINGS
PREP **25**	COOK **30**	MICRO.	HIGH	4

900 g (2 lb) monkfish, skinned and boned

25 g (1 oz) butter or margarine

1 large onion, skinned and chopped

1 garlic clove, skinned and crushed

450 g (1 lb) courgettes, trimmed and sliced

30 ml (2 level tbsp) plain flour

15 ml (1 level tbsp) paprika

150 ml (¼ pint) dry white wine

150 ml (¼ pint) fish or chicken stock

225 g (8 oz) tomatoes, skinned, seeded, and chopped

15 ml (1 level tbsp) fresh or dried basil

salt and pepper

1 Cut the fish into 5 cm (2 inch) pieces.

2 Place the butter or margarine in a large bowl and microwave on HIGH for 45 seconds or until melted. Add the onion and garlic and microwave on HIGH for 5–7 minutes or until soft, stirring once. Add the courgettes, cover and microwave on HIGH for 2 minutes.

3 Stir in the flour, paprika, wine, stock, tomatoes, basil and seasoning. Microwave on HIGH for 5 minutes or until boiling, then continue to microwave on HIGH for a further 5 minutes.

4 Add the fish, cover and microwave on HIGH for 10 minutes or until the fish is tender, stirring once.

Serve with sauté potatoes and a green salad.

COOK'S TIP

For a more economical dish, choose another firm white fish such as cod or haddock.

Fish Steaks in Tomato Sauce

TIMES		METHOD	SETTINGS	SERVINGS
PREP **10**	COOK **16**	MICRO.	HIGH	4

15 ml (1 tbsp) vegetable oil

100 g (4 oz) mushrooms, wiped and sliced

1 small onion, skinned and finely chopped

1 garlic clove, skinned and crushed

397 g (14 oz) can chopped tomatoes

salt and pepper

4 white fish steaks or fillets, each weighing 100 g (4 oz)

1 Mix the oil, mushrooms, onion and garlic together in a shallow dish and microwave on HIGH for 5 minutes or until soft, stirring once.

2 Stir in the tomatoes and seasoning. Microwave on HIGH for 5 minutes or until bubbling.

3 Arrange the fish in a single layer in the casserole, spooning the sauce over the top. Microwave on HIGH for 6 minutes or until the fish flakes, turning once.

Serve with a green vegetable and boiled potatoes.

COOK'S TIP

To ensure even cooking, arrange the fish with the thinnest part towards the centre of the dish.

Lamb and cabbage parcels (Meat) *opposite*

Scampi Provençal

TIMES		METHOD	SETTINGS	SERVINGS
PREP.	COOK	MICRO.	HIGH	2
10	18			

25 g (1 oz) butter or margarine

1 garlic clove, skinned and crushed

2 large onions, skinned and chopped

227 g (8 oz) can tomatoes, drained and chopped

45 ml (3 tbsp) dry white wine

salt and pepper

450 g (1 lb) frozen scampi, thawed

30 ml (2 tbsp) chopped fresh parsley

1 Place the butter or margarine in a medium bowl and microwave on HIGH for 45 seconds or until melted. Stir in the garlic and onion and microwave on HIGH for 5–7 minutes or until soft, stirring once.

2 Add the tomatoes, wine and seasoning and microwave on HIGH for 5 minutes.

3 Stir in the scampi and parsley. Cover and microwave on HIGH for 5 minutes or until the fish is tender, stirring once.

Serve with rice.

COOK'S TIP

To thaw the scampi in the microwave, arrange on a plate in a circle, cover with absorbent kitchen paper and microwave on LOW for 3 minutes. Leave to stand for 5 minutes, then microwave on LOW for a further 3 minutes. Leave to stand for another 5 minutes.

Luxury Fish Pie

TIMES		METHOD	SETTINGS	SERVINGS
PREP.	COOK	MICRO. CONVEN.	HIGH	4
35	30			

700 g (1½ lb) potatoes, peeled and diced

salt and pepper

75 g (3 oz) butter or margarine

2 eggs, separated

450 g (1 lb) firm white fish, such as cod

450 g (1 lb) smoked haddock

45 ml (3 level tbsp) plain flour

300 ml (10 fl oz) single cream

100 g (4 oz) button mushrooms, sliced

100 g (4 oz) peeled prawns

30 ml (2 tbsp) chopped fresh parsley

30 ml (2 level tbsp) freshly grated Parmesan cheese

1 Cook the potatoes conventionally in boiling salted water until tender. Drain and mash with 50 g (2 oz) butter or margarine and the egg yolks.

2 Arrange the fish in a shallow dish and add 100 ml (4 fl oz) water. Cover and microwave on HIGH for 6 minutes, turning the dish once. Leave to stand, covered, for 3 minutes, then drain, reserving the liquid, and flake the fish.

3 Whisk the egg whites until stiff and fold into the mashed potatoes. Season to taste.

4 Place the remaining butter or margarine in a large shallow flameproof dish and microwave on HIGH for 45 seconds or until melted. Stir in the flour and microwave on HIGH for 30 seconds. Gradually whisk in the cream and the reserved cooking liquid. Microwave on HIGH for 3 minutes, whisking occasionally, until thick and smooth.

5 Stir in the flaked fish, mushrooms, prawns and parsley. Season and microwave on HIGH for 2 minutes or until hot.

6 Spoon or pipe the mashed potatoes around the edge of the dish. Sprinkle with cheese and grill until golden.

Serve with a green vegetable.

Dutch Fish Pancakes

TIMES		METHOD	SETTINGS	SERVINGS
PREP. **20**	COOK **18**	MICRO. CONVEN.	HIGH	4

8 pancakes (see page 49)

For the filling:

450 g (1 lb) smoked haddock fillet

25 g (1 oz) butter or margarine

25 g (1 oz) plain flour

300 ml (½ pint) milk

salt and pepper

15 ml (1 tbsp) lemon juice

175 g (6 oz) Gouda cheese, finely grated

chopped fresh parsley or snipped chives, to garnish

1 To make the filling, arrange the fish in a shallow dish, placing the thicker end towards the edge of the dish. Pour over 150 ml (¼ pint) water, cover and microwave on HIGH for 6 minutes or until tender. Leave to stand, covered.

2 Place the butter or margarine in a medium bowl and microwave on HIGH for 45 seconds or until melted. Stir in the flour and microwave on HIGH for 30 seconds, then gradually whisk in the milk. Microwave on HIGH for 3 minutes or until boiling and thickened, whisking occasionally. Season lightly, remembering that the fish may be salty, and beat in the lemon juice and 150 g (5 oz) cheese.

3 Drain the fish, remove the skin and flake the flesh, discarding any bones.

4 Mix the fish with one-third of the sauce. Divide the filling between the pancakes, spooning it along the centres. Roll up and arrange in a deep flameproof dish, seam side down.

5 Spoon over the remaining sauce. Cover and microwave on HIGH for 6 minutes or until bubbling.

6 Sprinkle with the remaining cheese and grill under a hot grill until golden brown. Serve, sprinkled with parsley or chives.

Serve with a crisp green salad.

Tuna Fish Pie

TIMES		METHOD	SETTINGS	SERVINGS
PREP. **20**	COOK **38**	MICRO. CONVEN.	HIGH	4

330 g (11.6 oz) packet frozen puff pastry, thawed

little beaten egg, for glazing

For the filling:

25 g (1 oz) butter or margarine

225 g (8 oz) button mushrooms, wiped and sliced

45 ml (3 level tbsp) plain flour

150 ml (¼ pint) milk

finely grated rind and juice of 1 lemon

half a bunch of watercress, washed, trimmed and finely chopped

two 198 g (7 oz) cans tuna, drained and flaked

salt and pepper

1 Place the butter or margarine in a medium bowl and microwave on HIGH for 45 seconds or until melted. Add the mushrooms and microwave on HIGH for 2 minutes or until beginning to soften.

2 Stir in the flour and microwave on HIGH for 30 seconds. Gradually whisk in the milk and microwave on HIGH for 5 minutes or until boiling and thickened, whisking occasionally. Stir in the lemon rind, lemon juice, watercress and tuna. Season to taste and leave to cool.

3 Roll out the pastry to a 30.5 cm (12 inch) square. Transfer to a wetted baking sheet.

4 Spread the tuna mixture in the centre of the pastry. Brush the edges with water and bring each pastry corner to the centre to look like a sealed envelope.

5 Brush with beaten egg and bake conventionally in a 220°C (425°F) mark 7 oven for about 30 minutes until golden brown. Serve hot.

Serve with a salad made using the other half of the watercress bunch, thinly sliced onion and diced cucumber. Top with sieved hard boiled egg.

Soufflé Fish Ring

TIMES		METHOD	SETTINGS	SERVINGS
PREP **30**	COOK **12**	MICRO.	HIGH	4

450 g (1 lb) firm white fish fillet, such as cod or haddock

50 g (2 oz) fresh breadcrumbs

3 eggs, separated

50 g (2 oz) Cheddar cheese, grated

salt and pepper

225 g (8 oz) carrots, cut into matchsticks

half a cucumber, cut into matchsticks

75 g (3 oz) butter, cut into small pieces

finely grated rind and juice of 1 lemon

45 ml (3 tbsp) finely chopped fresh parsley or snipped chives

1 Skin the fish and place the flesh in a blender or food processor together with the breadcrumbs, egg yolks and cheese. Season to taste and mix until very smooth.

2 Whisk the egg whites until stiff and fold into the fish mixture.

3 Spoon into a 1.7–2.3 litre (3–4 pint) ring mould and microwave on HIGH for 5–6 minutes or until the fish flakes, turning once. Leave to stand, covered.

4 Place the carrots in a small bowl, cover and microwave on HIGH for 3 minutes. Add the cucumber and microwave on HIGH for 2 minutes. Set aside and keep hot.

5 Place the butter in a small bowl and microwave on HIGH for 45 seconds or until melted. Stir in the lemon rind, lemon juice, seasoning and parsley or chives.

6 Loosen the edges of the fish mould with a palette knife and unmould on to a serving plate. Fill the centre with some of the julienne vegetables. Spoon over some of the lemon butter. Serve with the remaining vegetables and pass the sauce separately.

Serve with boiled new potatoes.

Cheesy Baked Fish

TIMES		METHOD	SETTINGS	SERVINGS
PREP **20**	COOK **28**	MICRO. CONVEN.	HIGH	4

100 g (4 oz) streaky bacon, rinded and chopped

1 small onion, skinned and finely chopped

2 celery sticks, trimmed and finely chopped

75 g (3 oz) butter or margarine

100 g (4 oz) fresh breadcrumbs

450 ml (¾ pint) milk

700 g (1½ lb) cod fillet, skinned

50 g (2 oz) plain flour

pinch of mustard powder

175 g (6 oz) Cheshire cheese, finely grated

salt and pepper

1 Place the bacon, onion, celery and 25 g (1 oz) butter or margarine in a medium bowl and microwave on HIGH for 5–7 minutes or until soft, stirring once. Stir in the breadcrumbs and 30 ml (2 tbsp) milk.

2 Cut the fish in half crossways. Place one piece in a deep flameproof rectangular dish and spread with the bacon mixture. Cover with the remaining fish.

3 Place the remaining butter or margarine in a medium bowl and microwave on HIGH for 45 seconds or until melted. Stir in the flour and mustard and microwave on HIGH for 30 seconds. Gradually whisk in the remaining milk and microwave on HIGH for 3 minutes or until thick and smooth, whisking occasionally. Stir in 150 g (5 oz) cheese and season to taste with salt and pepper.

4 Pour the sauce over the fish and sprinkle with the remaining cheese. Cover and microwave on HIGH for 12–15 minutes or until the fish is tender.

5 Place the dish under a hot grill and leave until the top is golden brown.

Poultry

The best poultry and game for cooking in the microwave are boned rolled joints and birds or joints (such as thighs) which are an even, compact shape. They will cook more evenly and require less attention than whole birds or joints (like drumsticks) with protruding, bony ends. Whole birds should be well trussed before cooking. There is a good selection of turkey cuts ideal for microwaving such as turkey steaks and boned rolled joints. Turkey fillets and boneless chicken breasts cook quickly and evenly in the microwave.

Of course, other poultry joints can be successfully microwaved but they will need more frequent repositioning and careful watching during cooking so that parts of the joint do not overcook. If necessary, wing tips or other protruding pieces can be shielded with small, smooth pieces of foil, though this is unnecessary when joints are cooked in a sauce.

Because of the speed of cooking, boilers do not cook long enough to become tender in the microwave. Choose young game birds and avoid using boiling fowls or casserole hens which need long slow cooking. Unless cut into small boned pieces or minced, tough birds are best cooked conventionally though they reheat very well in the microwave. They can also be cooked in the conventional way, and then added to a sauce made in the microwave.

Browning
When preparing chicken and other birds for casseroles and stews, brown the skin to give it a more attractive appearance. Small pieces of poultry can be browned in a preheated browning dish and then cooked in the same dish along with the rest of the casserole ingredients. Depending on the dish being cooked, poultry can be grilled or browned and seared in a frying pan and then cooked in the microwave or it can be finished off under the grill. Breadcrumbed pieces of poultry can be cooked in the microwave, then grilled to give them a crispy coating.

Skinning poultry before cooking allows other flavours to penetrate the meat more easily and makes browning unnecessary. Skinned poultry takes slightly less time to microwave than poultry with skin.

Cooking
Start cooking whole birds breast side down and turn them over halfway through cooking; large birds will need to be turned 3 or 4 times during microwaving. Place joints skin side down to start cooking and turn over halfway.

Leave poultry and game to stand for 10 minutes after cooking, loosely covered or tented with foil. An accompanying sauce can be made during this standing time.

Test to see if the poultry is cooked in the conventional way, by piercing the thickest part of the chicken or turkey with a sharp knife. The juices will run clear when the meat is cooked. For other poultry and game, the meat should be tender and the joints should easily pull apart.

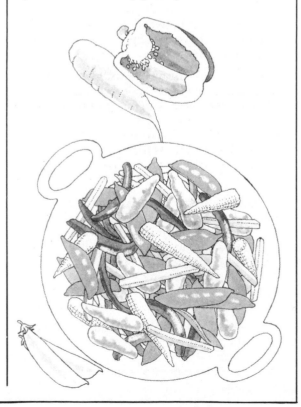

Artichoke-Stuffed Chicken Breasts

TIMES		METHOD	SETTINGS	SERVINGS
PREP	COOK			
35	14	MICRO.	HIGH	4

4 chicken breasts, skinned and boned

For the sauce:

25 g (1 oz) butter or margarine

30 ml (2 level tbsp) plain flour

150 ml (5 fl oz) single cream

150 ml (¼ pint) chicken stock

15 ml (1 tbsp) chopped fresh parsley

For the stuffing:

200 g (7 oz) can artichoke hearts, drained

50 g (2 oz) Cheddar cheese, grated

15 ml (1 tbsp) snipped chives

25 g (1 oz) fresh breadcrumbs

little beaten egg

salt and pepper

1 To make the stuffing, finely chop the artichoke hearts and mix with the cheese, chives, breadcrumbs and enough egg to bind. Season to taste with salt and pepper.

2 Using a mallet or rolling pin, flatten the chicken breasts between two sheets of dampened greaseproof paper or cling film until they are 0.5 cm (¼ inch) thick.

3 Spread the stuffing over the meat, roll up and secure with wooden cocktail sticks. Place in a shallow casserole, seam side up. Cover and microwave on HIGH for 5 minutes. Turn over, re-cover and microwave on HIGH for 5 minutes, or until the chicken is tender. Leave to stand, covered.

4 Place the butter or margarine in a medium bowl and microwave on HIGH for 45 seconds or until melted. Whisk in the flour and microwave on HIGH for 30 seconds, then gradually whisk in the cream and chicken stock. Microwave on HIGH for 3 minutes, stirring once. Do not allow to boil. Stir in the parsley and season.

5 Remove the wooden cocktail sticks and pour the sauce over the meat.

Serve with new potatoes and a green vegetable.

Chicken with Apple and Mustard Sauce

TIMES		METHOD	SETTINGS	SERVINGS
PREP	COOK			
25	31	MICRO.	HIGH	4

8 chicken thighs, skinned

60–75 ml (4–5 level tbsp) prepared English mustard

25 g (1 oz) butter or margarine

2 medium onions, skinned and thinly sliced

1 medium cooking apple, peeled, cored and sliced

salt and pepper

15 ml (1 level tbsp) plain flour

150 ml (¼ pint) chicken stock

chopped fresh parsley, to garnish

1 Prick the chicken with a fork and spread generously with the mustard. Place in a non-metal dish, cover and refrigerate for several hours or overnight.

2 Place the butter or margarine in a large shallow casserole and microwave on HIGH for 45 seconds or until melted. Add the onion and apple and stir well. Microwave on HIGH for 5–7 minutes or until the onion is soft. Season to taste with salt and pepper.

3 Arrange the chicken on top of the onion and apple, bone side up. Cover and microwave on HIGH for 10 minutes. Turn the chicken over, leave uncovered and microwave on HIGH for a further 10 minutes or until tender. Transfer the chicken to a heated serving dish and keep hot.

4 Sprinkle the flour over the onions and apple and mix well. Microwave on HIGH for 1 minute, then gradually stir in the chicken stock. Season to taste and microwave on HIGH for 2 minutes or until thickened and smooth.

5 Pour the sauce over the chicken and garnish with the parsley. Serve at once.

Serve with baked potatoes.

Pigeons in Rich Tomato Sauce

TIMES PREP.	COOK	METHOD	SETTINGS	SERVINGS
20	55	MICRO. CONVEN.	MEDIUM HIGH	4

4 oven-ready pigeons

60 ml (4 tbsp) vegetable oil

4 slices day-old bread, crusts removed

For the sauce:

100 g (4 oz) streaky bacon, rinded and finely chopped

2 medium onions, skinned and chopped

3 garlic cloves, skinned and crushed

60 ml (4 level tbsp) soft brown sugar

90 ml (6 level tbsp) tomato purée

90 ml (6 tbsp) dry sherry

two 397 g (14 oz) cans tomatoes

salt and pepper

60 ml (4 tbsp) double cream

1 To make the sauce, place the bacon in a large bowl and microwave on HIGH for 4 minutes or until the fat runs. Stir in the onions, garlic and sugar and microwave on HIGH for 5 minutes, stirring once. Add the tomato purée, sherry and tomatoes. Season to taste and microwave on HIGH for 10 minutes.

2 Place the pigeons breast side down in a large, deep casserole. Pour over the sauce. Cover and microwave on HIGH for 20 minutes, then turn the pigeons over, re-cover and microwave on MEDIUM for 10 minutes.

3 Heat the oil in a frying pan and fry the bread slices on both sides until crisp.

4 Arrange the fried bread on a heated serving dish, put a pigeon on top of each slice and keep hot.

5 Purée the sauce with the cream in a blender or food processor and pour into a serving jug or bowl. Heat through on MEDIUM for 1 minute. Spoon a little sauce over the pigeons and serve the remainder separately.

Serve with mashed potatoes and a green vegetable.

Chinese-Style Chicken with Vegetables

TIMES PREP.	COOK	METHOD	SETTINGS	SERVINGS
25	11	MICRO.	HIGH	4

450 g (1 lb) boned chicken breasts, skinned

30 ml (2 tbsp) dry sherry

15 ml (1 tbsp) soy sauce

100 g (4 oz) carrots, peeled

1 large green pepper, seeded and thinly sliced

1 large red pepper, seeded and thinly sliced

100 g (4 oz) mange-tout, trimmed

50 g (2 oz) baby corn-on-the-cobs

2 large courgettes, trimmed and sliced

pepper

1 Cut the chicken into 1 cm (½ inch) wide strips and place in a medium casserole.

2 Mix the sherry and soy sauce together, add to the chicken and leave to marinate for 30 minutes.

3 Cut the carrots into strips about 5 cm (2 inches) long and 1 cm (½ inch) wide. Put into a polythene bag together with the green and red peppers, mange-tout and courgettes. Loosely fold over the top of the bag and microwave on HIGH for 2 minutes.

3 Mix the corn with the chicken. Three-quarters cover and microwave on HIGH for 6 minutes or until tender, stirring twice.

4 Stir in the vegetables. Season to taste with pepper and microwave on HIGH for 3 minutes or until the vegetables are tender but still firm.

Serve with boiled rice and extra soy sauce.

Chicken Roulades with Mushrooms in Cream

TIMES	
PREP 40	COOK 41

METHOD
MICRO.

SETTINGS
HIGH

SERVINGS
(4)

350 g (12 oz) button mushrooms, wiped

1 medium onion, skinned and finely chopped

2 celery sticks, trimmed and finely chopped

1 garlic clove, skinned and crushed

30 ml (2 tbsp) vegetable oil

50 g (2 oz) walnuts, finely chopped

25 g (1 oz) fresh breadcrumbs

finely grated rind and juice of 1 lemon

5 ml (1 level tsp) dried thyme

15 ml (1 tbsp) chopped fresh parsley

salt and pepper

4 chicken breasts, skinned and boned

25 g (1 oz) butter or margarine

15 ml (1 level tbsp) plain flour

150 ml (5 fl oz) whipping cream

50 ml (2 fl oz) dry white wine

1 Slice 225 g (8 oz) mushrooms and set aside for the sauce. Finely chop the rest and place in a medium bowl.

2 Add half the onion to the bowl along with the celery, garlic and 15 ml (1 tbsp) oil. Microwave on HIGH for 10 minutes or until the onion and celery are soft, stirring once. Stir in the walnuts, breadcrumbs, lemon rind, herbs and enough lemon juice to bind the mixture. Season to taste.

3 Using a meat mallet or rolling pin, flatten the chicken breasts between two sheets of dampened greaseproof paper or cling film to a thickness of 0.5 cm (¼ inch). Spread the stuffing over the chicken, roll up and secure with wooden cocktail sticks.

4 Place the chicken seam side up on a microwave roasting rack. Brush with half the remaining oil and microwave on HIGH for 16 minutes or until tender. Turn the chicken over halfway through cooking time and brush with the remaining oil. Leave to stand covered.

5 In a large bowl, microwave the butter or margarine on HIGH for 45 seconds or until melted. Stir in the remaining onion and microwave on HIGH for 5–7 minutes or until soft. Add the reserved mushrooms and continue to microwave for a further 7 minutes, stirring once.

6 Stir in the flour and microwave on HIGH for 30 seconds. Gradually stir in the cream and wine and microwave on HIGH for 8 minutes or until thickened and smooth, stirring occasionally. Season to taste.

7 Place the chicken in a shallow dish. Spoon over the sauce and microwave on HIGH for 2 minutes or until heated through.

Serve with boiled rice.

COOK'S TIP

This dish is equally successful made with turkey breasts instead of chicken.

Walnut pie (Desserts) *opposite*
Haddock mousse and monkfish in white wine (Fish) *overleaf*

Indonesian Spiced Turkey

TIMES		METHOD	SETTINGS	SERVINGS
PREP.	COOK			
25	23	MICRO.	HIGH	6

900 g (2 lb) boneless turkey fillet

7.5 ml (1½ level tsp) ground cumin

7.5 ml (1½ level tsp) ground coriander

2.5 ml (½ level tsp) turmeric

2.5 ml (½ level tsp) ground ginger

30 ml (2 tbsp) lemon juice

284 g (10 oz) natural yogurt

salt and pepper

1 large onion, skinned and chopped

15 ml (1 tbsp) vegetable oil

30 ml (2 level tbsp) plain flour

45 ml (3 level tbsp) desiccated coconut

chopped fresh coriander, to garnish

1 Cut the turkey breast into bite-sized pieces, making sure they are all the same size.

2 In a large bowl, mix the spices, lemon juice and yogurt together and season to taste. Add the turkey and coat thoroughly with the sauce. Cover and refrigerate for at least 3 hours or overnight. Stir once or twice during marinating.

3 Place the onion and oil in a large casserole, mix together and microwave on HIGH for 5–7 minutes or until soft. Stir in the flour and coconut and microwave on HIGH for 1 minute.

4 Add the turkey and yogurt mixture, cover and microwave on HIGH for 15 minutes, or until the turkey is tender, stirring occasionally. Sprinkle with coriander and serve.

Serve with boiled rice.

Devilled Turkey Wings

TIMES		METHOD	SETTINGS	SERVINGS
PREP.	COOK		HIGH	
10	14	MICRO.	MEDIUM	2

2 turkey wings, skinned

30 ml (2 level tbsp) mustard powder

30 ml (2 tbsp) Worcestershire sauce

30 ml (2 level tbsp) soft dark brown sugar

salt and pepper

1 Using a sharp knife, make 1 cm (½ inch) deep incisions all over the turkey wings.

2 Blend the mustard powder, Worcestershire sauce and brown sugar together and season with salt and pepper. Rub the mixture into the turkey. Cover and refrigerate for at least 3 hours or overnight.

3 Calculate the cooking time allowing 14 minutes per 450 g (1 lb) turkey. Place the turkey on a roasting rack, cover and microwave on HIGH for 5 minutes, then microwave on MEDIUM for the remaining time except for the final 5 minutes. For this time, uncover the turkey and microwave on HIGH.

Serve with hot french bread.

COOK'S TIP

Buy whole turkey wings for this dish – not the smaller wing tips which have very little meat and are best reserved for stocks.

Glazed vegetables Provençal (Vegetables)
opposite

Turkey with Hazel Nut Sauce

TIMES		METHOD	SETTINGS	SERVINGS
PREP.	COOK	MICRO.	HIGH	4
10	14			

450 lb (1 lb) turkey breast fillets

25 g (1 oz) butter or margarine

60 ml (4 tbsp) sweet sherry

60 ml (4 tbsp) double cream

25 g (1 oz) hazel nuts, finely chopped

salt and pepper

paprika, to garnish

1 Cut the turkey fillets into 0.5 cm (¼ inch) slices.

2 Place the butter or margarine in a shallow casserole and microwave on HIGH for 45 seconds or until melted. Stir in the turkey slices and microwave on HIGH for 5–6 minutes or until just cooked, stirring once or twice.

3 Add the sherry, cream and hazel nuts. Stir well and microwave on HIGH for 7 minutes or until boiling, stirring occasionally. Sprinkle with paprika and serve.

Serve with brown rice and a green salad.

Spicy Oriental Turkey

TIMES		METHOD	SETTINGS	SERVINGS
PREP.	COOK	MICRO.	HIGH	4
15	10			

700 g (1½ lb) boneless turkey breast

1 egg white

45 ml (3 level tbsp) cornflour

pinch of salt

15 ml (1 tbsp) vegetable oil

30 ml (2 level tbsp) soft brown sugar

30 ml (2 tbsp) cider vinegar

45–60 ml (3–4 tbsp) sweet chilli sauce

50 g (2 oz) roasted shelled peanuts, coarsely chopped

1 bunch of spring onions, trimmed and sliced

1 Cut the turkey breast into 2.5 cm (1 inch) cubes.

2 In a medium bowl, whisk the egg white, cornflour and salt together. Add the turkey and stir to coat thoroughly.

3 Place the oil in a large bowl and microwave on HIGH for 1 minute. Stir in the turkey and microwave on HIGH for 6 minutes, stirring once.

4 Blend the sugar, vinegar and chilli sauce together and add to the bowl with the peanuts and spring onions. Microwave on HIGH for 3 minutes or until the turkey is tender.

Serve with Chinese noodles.

COOK'S TIP

This dish tastes best made with sweet chilli sauce but for a hotter flavour, use hot chilli sauce.

Peking-Style Duck

TIMES		METHOD	SETTINGS	SERVINGS
PREP. 60	COOK 80	MICRO. CONVEN.	HIGH	4

1 bunch of spring onions, washed and trimmed

½ cucumber

2 kg (4–4½ lb) oven-ready duckling

soy sauce

100 ml (4 fl oz) hoi sin sauce

For the pancakes:

450 g (1 lb) plain flour

pinch of salt

15 ml (1 tbsp) vegetable oil plus extra for brushing

1 Trim off the root end of the spring onions, and trim the green leaves down to about 5 cm (2 inches). Skin, then cut twice lengthways to within 2.5 cm (1 inch) off the end. Place in a bowl of iced water and refrigerate for 1–2 hours or until the onion curls. Cut the cucumber into 5 cm (2 inch) fingers.

2 To make the pancakes, place the flour and salt in a large bowl. Gradually mix in 15 ml (1 tbsp) oil and 375 ml (13 fl oz) boiling water, stirring vigorously with a wooden spoon. When the dough is slightly cool, shape into a ball and turn on to a lightly floured surface. Knead for about 5 minutes to make a soft smooth dough. Leave to stand in a bowl for 30 minutes covered with a damp cloth or cling film.

3 Cut the dough in half and shape each half into a roll 40 cm (16 inches) long. Cut each roll into 16 even slices. On a lightly floured surface, roll out 2 slices of dough into circles about 7.5 cm (3 inches) across. Brush the tops with oil. Put the oiled surfaces together and roll out to a thin 15 cm (6 inch) circle. Repeat with the remaining dough to make a total of 16 pairs of pancakes.

4 Heat an ungreased frying pan or griddle and cook each pair of pancakes for about 1–2 minutes on each side, turning when air bubbles start to form. Remove from the frying pan and while they are still hot

separate the pancakes. Stack in a clean damp tea towel.

5 Pat the duck dry with absorbent kitchen paper. Calculate the cooking time at 10 minutes per 450 g (1 lb). Place the duck breast side down on a microwave roasting rack and brush with soy sauce.

6 Cover and microwave on HIGH for the calculated cooking time. Turn the duck over halfway through cooking, brush with soy sauce and continue to microwave on HIGH, uncovered, until the duck is tender. Leave the duck to stand, loosely covered with foil.

7 Grill the duck under a hot grill for about 2 minutes until golden brown and the skin is crisp on all sides.

8 Microwave the hoi sin sauce on HIGH for about 2 minutes until just bubbling.

9 Cut the duck into small pieces. Meanwhile, microwave the pancakes wrapped in the damp tea towel on HIGH for 2 minutes or until just warm.

10 Serve each person with 8 pancakes and some of the duck, including the skin. Hand the vegetables and sauce separately. To eat, spread a little sauce on a pancake and top with vegetables and duck. Roll up and eat with your fingers.

COOK'S TIP

The roasting rack must be placed in a deep dish to catch all the fat which runs out of the duck during cooking.

Duck with Peach Sauce

TIMES		METHOD	SETTINGS	SERVINGS
PREP	COOK	MICRO.	MEDIUM	
10	52	CONVEN.	HIGH	

4 duckling portions, each weighing about 300 g (11 oz)

30 ml (2 tbsp) soy sauce

For the sauce:

411 g (14½ oz) can peach slices in natural juice

15 ml (1 level tbsp) plain flour

15 ml (1 level tbsp) whole-grain mustard

salt and pepper

60 ml (4 level tbsp) peach chutney

1 Pat the duckling portions dry with absorbent kitchen paper. Place them skin side down on a microwave roasting rack and brush with half the soy sauce.

2 Cover and microwave on HIGH for 10 minutes. Switch to MEDIUM and microwave for 30 minutes, repositioning the portions once or twice. Turn the duckling skin side up and brush with the remaining soy sauce. Microwave on HIGH for 5 minutes or until tender.

3 Transfer the duckling to a hot grill and grill until the skins are crisp.

4 To make the sauce, drain the peaches, reserving the juice. Blend the juice with the flour and mustard in a serving jug or bowl and season to taste. Microwave on HIGH for 3 minutes or until thickened and smooth, stirring once or twice.

5 Put the peach slices in a blender or food processor and add the sauce. Blend until smooth and add to the flour and juice mixture. Stir in the chutney and microwave on HIGH for 2 minutes or until hot. Serve the duck with the sauce handed separately.

Serve with boiled potatoes and a green vegetable.

Braised Pheasant with Forcemeat Balls

TIMES		METHOD	SETTINGS	SERVINGS
PREP	COOK	MICRO.	HIGH	
20	35			

2 oven-ready pheasants, total weight about 2 kg (4 lb)

300 ml (½ pint) chicken stock

1 medium onion, skinned and chopped

15 ml (1 tbsp) brandy

15 ml (1 level tbsp) cornflour

60 ml (4 level tbsp) redcurrant jelly

15 ml (1 tbsp) lemon juice

For the forcemeat balls:

225 g (8 oz) pork sausagemeat

30 ml (2 tbsp) chopped fresh parsley

salt and pepper

30 ml (2 level tbsp) toasted wheatgerm

1 Pat the pheasants dry with absorbent kitchen paper. Using poultry shears, cut each pheasant along the breastbone and backbone, so it is cut in half.

2 Place the pheasants breast side down in a shallow casserole. Pour in the stock and add the onion. Cover and microwave on HIGH for 15 minutes.

3 Meanwhile, mix the sausagemeat and parsley together. Season to taste and shape into 8 balls. Roll each ball in the wheatgerm to coat all over.

4 Add the forcemeat balls to the casserole. Turn the pheasants over and microwave on HIGH, uncovered, for 15 minutes or until the pheasants are tender.

5 Using a slotted spoon, transfer the pheasant and forcemeat balls to a heated serving dish. Loosely cover and keep hot.

6 Blend the brandy, cornflour, redcurrant jelly and lemon juice together and add to the pan juices. Season to taste. Microwave on HIGH for 5 minutes or until thickened and smooth, stirring occasionally.

7 Pour a little sauce over the pheasant and hand the remaining separately.

Serve with game chips and green vegetables.

Meat

When it comes to cooking meat, use the microwave oven for those dishes it cooks best and cook others conventionally. So many of our favourite meat dishes are simply grilled or fried and you may find that you prefer to cook these conventionally and use the microwave for preparing a sauce and/or vegetables. Joints, however, can be roasted in about one-third of the time it takes to cook conventionally and they retain their juices well. A number of meat dishes incorporating a sauce and other vegetables are also ideal for microwave cooking.

A meal can be made in minutes, simply brown the meat in a browning dish then add the other ingredients. Because of the speed of cooking, tough cuts of meat do not have time to become tender, so some stews, especially beef stews, are best cooked conventionally and the microwave used for reheating them. Stews are also ideal for batch cooking for the freezer; they can be thawed and heated in the microwave.

Make sure the meat is cut into even-sized cubes or strips and trim off any excess fat. Fat melts more quickly in the microwave than with conventionally cooked meat and should be drained off during microwaving, otherwise the fat may splatter and cooking will be slowed down because the microwaves are attracted to the fat more than the meat.

Test meat to see if it is cooked by using a meat thermometer or by piercing the thickest part of the meat with a sharp knife to see if it is tender. If using a microwave meat thermometer or probe, remember that the fat in the meat becomes very hot and if the thermometer or probe pierces a piece of fat the reading could be inaccurate. Testing with a knife is easier and more accurate.

All meat, even meat which is part of a casserole, needs to stand after cooking. Cover the meat with foil, shiny side down. During this time, vegetables and sauces can be prepared. With casseroles, either transfer the meat to a heated serving dish or pour off the pan juices to make a sauce from the cooking liquid.

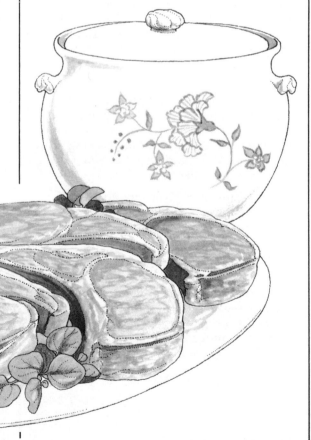

Beef and Mushroom Lasagne

TIMES		METHOD	SETTINGS	SERVINGS
PREP. 30	COOK 41	MICRO. CONVEN.	HIGH	4

175 g (6 oz) lasagne

45 ml (3 tbsp) vegetable oil

salt and pepper

300 ml (½ pint) white sauce (see page 113)

100 g (4 oz) Cheddar cheese, grated

For the meat sauce:

1 medium onion, skinned and finely chopped

450 g (1 lb) minced fresh beef

30 ml (2 level tbsp) plain flour

30 ml (2 level tsp) dried basil

397 g (14 oz) can chopped tomatoes

150 ml (¼ pint) hot beef stock

175 g (6 oz) mushrooms, wiped and sliced

1 Place the lasagne in a 5 cm (2 inch) deep rectangular casserole. Spoon over 5 ml (1 tsp) oil and add 900 ml (1½ pint) boiling water and a pinch of salt. Cover and microwave on HIGH for 9 minutes. Leave to stand for 15 minutes, then drain and rinse.

2 To make the sauce, mix the remaining oil and the onion in a medium bowl. Microwave on HIGH for 3 minutes, stirring once. Add the meat, breaking up any large pieces, and microwave on HIGH for 5 minutes, stirring once.

3 Stir in the flour, basil, tomatoes, stock and mushrooms. Season to taste with salt and pepper. Microwave on HIGH for 20 minutes, stirring once.

4 Layer the lasagne and meat sauce in the casserole dish, finishing with a layer of sauce. Pour over the white sauce and microwave on HIGH for 2 minutes or until heated through. Sprinkle with the cheese, and place under a hot grill until bubbling and the cheese is melted.

Serve with a green salad and hot garlic bread.

Chilli Con Carne

TIMES		METHOD	SETTINGS	SERVINGS
PREP. 10	COOK 48	MICRO. CONVEN.	HIGH	8

1 large onion, skinned and chopped

1 green pepper, seeded and cut into strips

15 ml (1 tbsp) vegetable oil

700 g (1½ lb) minced fresh beef

397 g (14 oz) can chopped tomatoes

30 ml (2 level tbsp) tomato purée

15 ml (1 tbsp) red wine vinegar

5 ml (1 level tsp) soft dark brown sugar

5–10 ml (1–2 level tsp) chilli powder

30 ml (2 level tbsp) ground cumin

salt and pepper

439 g (15½ oz) can red kidney beans, drained

1 In a large bowl, stir together the onion, pepper and oil. Microwave on HIGH for 5 minutes or until soft, stirring once. Add the beef, breaking up any large pieces. Microwave on HIGH for 6–8 minutes or until the meat starts to change colour, stirring once.

2 Mix together the tomatoes, tomato purée, vinegar, sugar and spices. Season to taste and stir into the meat. Cover and microwave on HIGH for 30 minutes, stirring once.

3 Add the beans, re-cover and microwave on HIGH for 5 minutes.

Serve with rice and a green salad.

COOK'S TIP

Chilli con carne reheats especially well; the flavours will develop and become more mellow if made in advance and then reheated.

Onion-Topped Meatloaf

TIMES		METHOD	SETTINGS	SERVINGS
PREP. 20	COOK 35	MICRO.	HIGH	6

15 ml (1 tbsp) vegetable oil

1 garlic clove, skinned and crushed

2 large onions, skinned and thinly sliced

2 celery sticks, finely chopped

2 eggs

60 ml (4 level tbsp) tomato purée

700 g (1½ lb) minced fresh beef

100 g (4 oz) fresh breadcrumbs

45 ml (3 tbsp) chopped fresh parsley

15 ml (1 tbsp) chopped fresh basil

salt and pepper

1 Place the oil, garlic and onions in a medium bowl and microwave on HIGH for 5–7 minutes or until soft, stirring twice.

2 Using a fork, transfer half the onions to the base of a 1.5 litre (2½ pint) microwave ring mould.

3 Stir the celery into the remaining onions and microwave on HIGH for 3 minutes or until soft.

4 Beat the eggs and tomato purée together in a large mixing bowl. Mix in the meat, breadcrumbs, parsley, basil and onion and celery mixture. Season to taste with salt and pepper.

5 Spoon into the ring mould, pressing the mixture down lightly. Microwave on HIGH for 20 minutes. Leave to stand for 5 minutes. Unmould on to a heated serving dish.

Serve with tomato and olive sauce (see page 114), boiled potatoes and a green vegetable.

Beef Wellington

TIMES		METHOD	SETTINGS	SERVINGS
PREP. 30	COOK 55	MICRO. CONVEN.	HIGH	6

900 g (2 lb) fillet of beef, about 18 cm (7 inches) across

vegetable oil, for brushing

25 g (1 oz) butter or margarine

225 g (8 oz) mushrooms, wiped and thinly sliced

100 g (4 oz) smooth liver pâté

368 g (13 oz) packet frozen puff pastry, thawed

beaten egg, to glaze

1 Tie the beef with string at 1 cm (½ inch) intervals and brush the ends with oil.

2 Heat a browning dish to maximum according to the manufacturer's instructions.

3 Quickly seal the beef all over, including the two ends. Microwave on HIGH for 4 minutes, turning the beef over halfway through the cooking time.

4 Place the butter or margarine in a medium bowl and microwave on HIGH for 45 seconds or until melted. Add the mushrooms and microwave on HIGH for 4 minutes or until soft. Leave to cool, then blend with the pâté.

5 Roll out the pastry to a 25.5 × 30.5 cm (10 × 12 inch) rectangle.

6 Spread the pâté mixture along the centre of the pastry. Place the meat on top. Brush the pastry edges with beaten egg and fold the edges over the meat, then seal.

7 Using two fish slices, transfer the beef and pastry to a wetted baking tray, placing it so that the pastry join is underneath. Fold the pastry ends under the meat. Cut leaves from the pastry trimmings, brush with beaten egg and decorate the top. Chill in the refrigerator until firm.

8 Brush the pastry with the remaining egg glaze. Cook conventionally at 220°C (425°F) mark 7 for 40 minutes or until golden brown. Cover with foil, half-way through the cooking time if pastry is over browning.

Pork and Leeks in Cream

TIMES PREP	COOK	METHOD	SETTINGS	SERVINGS
10	38	MICRO. CONVEN.	HIGH	4

50 g (2 oz) butter or margarine

225 g (8 oz) leeks, thickly sliced and washed

1 garlic clove, skinned and crushed

350 g (12 oz) pork tenderloin

60 ml (4 tbsp) dry white wine or vermouth

150 ml (5 fl oz) double cream

15 ml (1 level tbsp) whole-grain mustard

salt and pepper

1 Place half the butter or margarine in a medium shallow casserole and microwave on HIGH for 45 seconds or until melted. Toss in the leeks and garlic and microwave on HIGH for 5–7 minutes or until soft, stirring once.

2 Cut the pork diagonally into very thin slices. Fry the slices conventionally in the remaining butter or margarine until golden brown on both sides.

3 Arrange the meat on top of the leeks. Deglaze the frying pan with the wine or vermouth and pour the liquid over the meat.

4 Blend the cream and mustard together and pour it over the meat and season to taste. Cover and microwave on HIGH for 15 minutes. Leave to stand for 5 minutes.

Serve with rice or noodles.

Pork Chops with Peppers

TIMES PREP	COOK	METHOD	SETTINGS	SERVINGS
10	27	MICRO.	HIGH	4

1 large onion, skinned and sliced

1 large red pepper, seeded and sliced

15 ml (1 tbsp) vegetable oil

4 boneless pork chops

30 ml (2 level tbsp) paprika

150 ml (5 fl oz) double cream

salt and pepper

1 Mix the onion, red pepper and oil in a shallow casserole. Microwave on HIGH for 5–7 minutes or until soft, stirring once.

2 Arrange the pork chops in a single layer on top of the vegetables. Blend the paprika and cream together. Season to taste and pour it over the meat.

3 Cover and microwave on HIGH for 20 minutes or until the pork is tender.

Serve with a green salad.

COOK'S TIP

The pork chops do not need to be first browned because they are covered with cream and paprika.

Pork with Spring Vegetables

TIMES		METHOD	SETTINGS	SERVINGS
PREP. 15	COOK 42	MICRO.	HIGH	4

1 large onion, skinned and sliced

15 ml (1 tbsp) vegetable oil

4 boneless pork chops

1 large green or yellow pepper, seeded and sliced

225 g (8 oz) courgettes, sliced

15 ml (1 tbsp) finely chopped fresh sage or lemon thyme

salt and pepper

225 g (8 oz) tomatoes, skinned, seeded and quartered

1 Mix the onion and oil together in a casserole large enough to fit the chops in a single layer. Microwave on HIGH for 5–7 minutes or until soft, stirring once.

2 Arrange the chops on top of the onion and cover with the green or yellow pepper and courgettes. Sprinkle with the herbs and season to taste. Cover and microwave on HIGH for 20–25 minutes or until the chops are tender.

3 Arrange the tomato wedges on top and microwave on HIGH, uncovered, for 5 minutes. Leave to stand for 5 minutes.

Serve with boiled new potatoes.

Sweet and Sour Pork

TIMES		METHOD	SETTINGS	SERVINGS
PREP. 30	COOK 27	MICRO.	HIGH	6

30 ml (2 level tbsp) soft dark brown sugar

30 ml (2 level tbsp) cornflour

450 g (1 lb) pork tenderloin, cut into matchsticks

1 large onion, skinned and thinly sliced

2 garlic cloves, skinned and crushed

15 ml (1 tbsp) vegetable oil

30 ml (2 tbsp) soy sauce

50 ml (2 fl oz) cider vinegar

225 g (8 oz) carrots, peeled and cut into matchsticks

439 g (15½ oz) can pineapple chunks in natural juice, drained with juice reserved

1 large green pepper, seeded and cut into matchsticks

230 g (8 oz) can water chestnuts, drained and sliced (optional)

1 Place the sugar and cornflour in a large polythene bag and add the pork. Toss together to coat the pork all over.

2 Mix the onion, garlic and oil in a large bowl. Microwave on HIGH for 5–7 minutes or until soft, stirring once.

3 Stir in the pork along with any cornflour mixture left in the bag. Add the soy sauce, vinegar, carrots and pineapple juice. Three-quarters cover and microwave on HIGH for 12–15 minutes, until the pork is tender, stirring once.

4 Stir in the pineapple chunks, green pepper and water chestnuts, if using. Microwave on HIGH, uncovered, for 5 minutes.

Serve immediately with rice.

Pork Suprême

TIMES PREP	TIMES COOK	METHOD	SETTINGS	SERVINGS
30	37	MICRO. CONVEN.	HIGH	4

225 g (8 oz) carrots, peeled and sliced

3 celery sticks, trimmed and thinly sliced

15 ml (1 tbsp) vegetable oil

4 boneless pork chops

15 ml (1 level tbsp) prepared mustard

300 ml (½ pint) onion sauce (see page 113)

450 g (1 lb) potatoes, peeled and thinly sliced

15 g (½ oz) butter, softened

1 Mix the carrots, celery and oil together in a large shallow casserole. Microwave on HIGH for 5–7 minutes or until soft, stirring once.

2 Arrange the chops in a single layer on top. Mix the mustard with the onion sauce and pour it over the meat and vegetables.

3 Arrange the potato slices on top. Cover and microwave on HIGH for 30 minutes or until the meat is tender.

4 Spread the butter over the potatoes and grill under a hot grill until golden brown.

Serve with a green vegetable such as broccoli spears.

Lamb and Cabbage Parcels

TIMES PREP	TIMES COOK	METHOD	SETTINGS	SERVINGS
20	23	MICRO.	HIGH	4

8 medium cabbage leaves

450 g (1 lb) minced fresh lamb

1 small onion, skinned and finely chopped

1 garlic clove, skinned and crushed

30 ml (2 tbsp) chopped fresh mint

1.25 ml (¼ level tsp) ground cinnamon

100 g (4 oz) fresh breadcrumbs

salt and pepper

about 15 ml (1 tbsp) lemon juice

10 ml (2 level tsp) cornflour

397 g (14 oz) can chopped tomatoes, sieved

15 ml (1 level tbsp) soft light brown sugar

30 ml (2 tbsp) chopped fresh parsley

1 Cut out the centre stem of each cabbage leaf and place the leaves in a large shallow casserole. Cover and microwave on HIGH for 2–3 minutes or until the leaves are soft.

2 Mix the lamb, onion, garlic, mint, cinnamon, breadcrumbs and seasoning together with enough lemon juice to bind. Shape into 8 even-sized cigar-shaped rolls.

3 Wrap each roll in a cabbage leaf and place in the casserole, seam side down.

4 Mix the cornflour to a smooth paste with a little of the tomato liquid, add the remaining tomatoes, the sugar and parsley. Spoon the tomato mixture over the cabbage rolls, cover and microwave on HIGH for 20 minutes.

Serve with jacket potatoes.

COOK'S TIP

Frozen minced lamb can be used instead of fresh. To thaw, microwave on LOW for 8–10 minutes, then leave to stand for 10 minutes.

Minced beef may be used instead of the lamb.

Lamb with Mint and Yogurt

TIMES PREP 25	COOK 43	METHOD MICRO.	SETTINGS MEDIUM HIGH	SERVINGS 4

1.25 kg (2¾ lb) leg of lamb, boned

15ml (1 tbsp) vegetable oil

1 medium onion, skinned and sliced

3 bay leaves

75 ml (5 tbsp) white wine vinegar

salt and pepper

15 ml (1 level tbsp) cornflour

5 ml (1 level tsp) granulated sugar

142 g (5 oz) natural yogurt

45 ml (3 tbsp) chopped fresh mint

30 ml (2 tbsp) chopped fresh parsley

1 Cut the lamb into 2.5 cm (1 inch) cubes.

2 Place the oil, onion, bay leaves, vinegar and seasoning in a large casserole. Microwave on HIGH for about 5 minutes or until boiling. Add the lamb to the casserole, cover and microwave on MEDIUM for 30 minutes or until the meat is tender. Leave to stand for 5 minutes.

3 Meanwhile, mix the cornflour and sugar to a smooth paste with 15 ml (1 tbsp) water. Add to the pan, stirring well, and microwave on HIGH for about 3 minutes, stirring after each minute, until thickened. Stir in the yogurt, mint and parsley and season to taste.

Serve with noodles or rice.

Lamb Fricassee

TIMES PREP 20	COOK 50	METHOD MICRO.	SETTINGS MEDIUM HIGH	SERVINGS 4

700 g (1½ lb) boned shoulder of lamb

225 g (8 oz) carrots, cut into fingers

1 medium onion, skinned and sliced

finely grated rind of 1 lemon

150 ml (¼ pint) dry white wine

salt and pepper

225 g (8 oz) frozen peas

25 g (1 oz) butter

25 g (1 oz) plain flour

1 egg yolk

150 ml (5 fl oz) single cream

1 Cut the lamb into 2.5 cm (1 inch) cubes and place in a large casserole. Add the carrots, onion, lemon rind, wine and 300 ml (½ pint) water. Season to taste with salt and pepper. Microwave on HIGH for 6 minutes or until boiling, then microwave on MEDIUM for 30 minutes.

2 Add the peas and microwave for a further 3 minutes or until the peas are hot. Strain off the cooking liquid and reserve. Keep the meat and vegetables hot.

3 Place the butter in a medium bowl and microwave on HIGH for 45 seconds or until melted. Stir in the flour and microwave on HIGH for 30 seconds. Gradually whisk in the cooking liquid. Microwave on HIGH until boiling, then microwave on HIGH for a further 4 minutes, whisking after every minute, until thickened and smooth. Check seasoning.

4 Whisk the egg yolk and cream together and whisk into the sauce. Microwave on HIGH for 1 minute but do not allow to boil. Pour the sauce over the meat and vegetables and serve.

Serve with jacket potatoes or rice.

Barbecued Lamb

TIMES	METHOD	SETTINGS	SERVINGS
PREP 15 COOK 27	MICRO.	HIGH	6

1.25 kg–1.5 kg (2½–3 lb) leg of lamb, boned

150 ml (¼ pint) tomato ketchup

15 ml (1 level tbsp) soft light brown sugar

1 small onion, skinned and finely chopped

15 ml (1 tbsp) fresh rosemary, finely chopped

30 ml (2 tbsp) red wine vinegar

salt and pepper

1 With a sharp knife, score the meat on both sides in a diamond pattern. This ensures good penetration of the marinade when added. Tie the meat into a neat compact shape and place in a large shallow dish.

2 Combine all the remaining ingredients and season to taste. Pour the marinade over the meat. Cover and refrigerate overnight, turning the meat over at least once.

3 Place the meat on a roasting rack and microwave on HIGH for 7–8 minutes per 450 g (1 lb) or until cooked, turning at least once. The meat should still be pink in the centre. Serve cut into thick slices.

Serve with a crisp green salad.

COOK'S TIP

Cook the meat for 8–10 minutes for 450 g (1 lb) if you prefer the lamb well done.

Veal Stroganoff

TIMES	METHOD	SETTINGS	SERVINGS
PREP 15 COOK 31	MICRO.	MEDIUM HIGH	4

450 g (1 lb) veal escalopes

50 g (2 oz) butter or margarine

1 large onion, skinned and sliced

225 g (8 oz) mushrooms, wiped and sliced

150 ml (¼ pint) white wine or chicken stock

142 ml (5 fl oz) soured cream

30 ml (2 level tbsp) tomato purée

15 ml (1 level tbsp) whole-grain mustard

10 ml (2 level tsp) paprika

salt and pepper

1 egg yolk

1 Cut the veal into thin strips.

2 Place the butter or margarine in a medium casserole and microwave on HIGH for 45 seconds or until melted. Stir in the onion and microwave on HIGH for 5–7 minutes, or until soft, stirring once.

3 Stir in the veal, mushrooms and wine or stock. Cover and microwave on HIGH for 15 minutes or until tender, stirring once.

4 Mix the remaining ingredients together. Season to taste and add to the meat. Microwave on MEDIUM for 5 minutes, stirring after each minute until thickened. Do not allow to boil. Leave to stand for 3 minutes.

Serve with egg noodles and a green salad.

COOK'S TIP

This dish tastes equally good made with beef fillet instead of veal.

Veal Marengo

TIMES PREP | COOK	METHOD	SETTINGS	SERVINGS
30 | 27	MICRO.	HIGH	4

4 veal escalopes

4 thin slices of ham

15 ml (1 tbsp) vegetable oil

2 carrots, peeled and finely chopped

2 celery sticks, trimmed and chopped

1 medium onion, skinned and finely chopped

50 g (2 oz) streaky bacon, rinded and chopped

45 ml (3 level tbsp) plain flour

150 ml (¼ pint) hot chicken stock

397 g (14 oz) can chopped tomatoes

30 ml (2 tbsp) sherry

salt and pepper

100 g (4 oz) mushrooms, wiped and sliced

chopped fresh parsley, to garnish

1 Using a mallet or rolling pin, beat the veal escalopes between two sheets of dampened greaseproof paper until they are thin.

2 Place a slice of ham on each escalope and roll up. Secure with wooden cocktail sticks and arrange in a deep casserole.

3 Place the oil, vegetables and bacon in a medium bowl. Microwave on HIGH for 5 minutes, stirring once. Stir in the flour and microwave on HIGH for 30 seconds. Gradually stir in the stock. Microwave on HIGH for 2 minutes, stirring once.

4 Add the tomatoes, sherry, seasoning and mushrooms. Pour the sauce over the veal, cover and microwave on HIGH for 20 minutes. Remove the cocktail sticks and sprinkle with parsley.

Serve with rice and a green vegetable.

Glazed Bacon with Orange Sauce

TIMES PREP | COOK	METHOD	SETTINGS	SERVINGS
10 | 20	MICRO. CONVEN.	MEDIUM HIGH	4

700 g (1½ lb) boneless lean bacon joint

60 ml (4 level tbsp) orange marmalade

45 ml (3 level tbsp) soft dark brown sugar

2.5 ml (½ level tsp) ground cinnamon

4–5 drops Tabasco sauce

60 ml (4 tbsp) orange juice

1 Place the bacon in a roasting bag and fasten with string or an elastic band. Prick the bag with a fork and microwave on HIGH for 5 minutes. Turn the joint over and microwave on MEDIUM for 10 minutes.

2 Mix the marmalade, sugar, cinnamon and Tabasco together in a small bowl.

3 Remove the meat from the bag and place in a shallow dish. Remove the rind, if necessary. Score the fat in a diamond pattern and spoon over half the marmalade mixture.

4 Brown the meat under a preheated grill until golden, turning if necessary.

5 Add the orange juice to the remaining marmalade mixture and microwave on HIGH for about 1½ minutes until bubbling. Serve the sauce with the meat.

Serve with boiled potatoes and a leafy green vegetable.

COOK'S TIP

Remember, smoked bacon easily dries out and toughens when microwaved so for best results use unsmoked bacon and if salty, soak overnight in cold water.

Eastern Spiced Liver

TIMES **PREP** 15 / **COOK** 8	METHOD **MICRO.**	SETTINGS **HIGH**	SERVINGS **4**

25 g (1 oz) desiccated coconut

450 g (1 lb) lamb's liver

45 ml (3 tbsp) vegetable oil

2 medium onions, skinned and thinly sliced.

5 ml (1 level tsp) chilli powder

15 ml (1 level tbsp) ground coriander

5 ml (1 level tsp) paprika

2.5 ml (½ level tsp) turmeric

30 ml (2 level tbsp) plain flour

300 ml (½ pint) chicken stock

30 ml (2 level tbsp) mango chutney

salt and pepper

1 Place the coconut and 150 ml (¼ pint) water in a large bowl. Cover and microwave on HIGH for 5 minutes or until boiling. Leave to stand for 15 minutes, then strain, reserving the liquid.

2 Meanwhile, cut the liver into small thin strips.

3 In a large shallow dish, mix the oil, onions and spices together and microwave on HIGH for 5 minutes, stirring frequently, until the onion is slightly softened. Add the liver.

4 Stir in the flour and microwave on HIGH for 30 seconds. Gradually blend in the stock, coconut liquid, chutney and seasoning. Microwave on HIGH for 5–7 minutes or until the liver is tender.

Serve with poppadums and rice.

Cheddar Sausages

TIMES **PREP** 10 / **COOK** 23	METHOD **MICRO.**	SETTINGS **HIGH**	SERVINGS **4**

2 medium onions, skinned and sliced

15 ml (1 tbsp) vegetable oil

8 sausages

1 large cooking apple

For the sauce:

25 g (1 oz) butter or margarine

45 ml (3 level tbsp) plain flour

5 ml (1 level tsp) mustard powder

300 ml (½ pint) milk

30 ml (2 level tbsp) tomato ketchup

100 g (4 oz) mature Cheddar cheese, grated

1 Mix the onions and oil together in a round casserole. Cover and microwave on HIGH for 5–7 minutes or until soft. Arrange the sausages in a circle on top, ends to the centre.

2 Peel, quarter and core the apple and cut into 8 wedges. Tuck in between the sausages.

3 To make the sauce, place the butter or margarine in a measuring jug and microwave on HIGH for 45 seconds or until melted. Blend in the flour and mustard powder and microwave on HIGH for 30 seconds. Gradually whisk in the milk and microwave on HIGH for 5 minutes or until thick and smooth, stirring once or twice. Stir in the ketchup and cheese.

4 Pour the sauce over the sausages and microwave on HIGH for 10 minutes.

Serve with mashed potatoes and a green vegetable.

Advance preparation: the sauce can be made in advance and kept in the refrigerator; cover the surface with greaseproof paper to prevent a skin forming. Allow an extra 2–3 minutes microwaving in stage 4.

Vegetables

Whether cooking vegetables in the microwave or conventionally, they taste best when they are tender but still firm. When microwaving vegetables always underestimate cooking times and remember that they will continue to cook, and therefore continue to soften, for about 3–4 minutes once microwaving has stopped. Remove them from the oven and cover loosely with foil to keep them hot.

When preparing meals, use the microwave as much as possible for cooking vegetables. They retain their flavours and natural colours much better than they would if cooked conventionally. As they need very little added water for cooking there is less loss of nutrients. Usually 30–45 ml (2–3 tbsp) water is added per 450 g (1 lb) vegetables. Vegetables with a high water content such as marrows, courgettes, spinach and mushrooms need no additional water but root vegetables, which take longer than other vegetables to cook, will need more water. Vegetables, especially frozen ones, cook superbly in a roasting bag with just a little butter added. Always pierce the bag before microwaving.

Vegetables can be microwaved while the rest of the meal is being made ready to serve. And because vegetables can be cooked in their serving dish, there are no extra saucepans or serving dishes to heat. To help retain moisture during cooking, three-quarters cover the dish with cling film; stretch the cling film over the dish and fold one side back to allow some steam to escape and to allow for stirring. When removing the cling film, use a tea towel or oven gloves and peel back away from you to avoid steam burns.

Because vegetables can be reheated without altering their fresh flavours, vegetable casseroles can be prepared in advance. For those with a topping which should be browned under a grill, first reheat the casserole in the microwave, then place under the grill. Co-ordinate cooking by making the sauce in advance in the microwave, cooking the vegetables then topping with the sauce and reheating in the microwave. Cook vegetables when a roast joint is left to stand after microwaving. Grill or fry chops and steaks in the conventional way and at the same time cook the vegetables in the microwave.

Preparing vegetables
To ensure that vegetables cook evenly, cut them to a uniform size. Remove any tough stems from broccoli and cauliflower as well as the tough cores from cabbage. Arrange the thicker or tougher parts of vegetables towards the outside of the dish where microwaving is more intense. Stalked vegetables like asparagus and broccoli should be placed with the stem ends towards the outside.

Salt tends to toughen vegetables during microwaving. Salt vegetables after cooking or if necessary mix the salt with the water before adding the vegetables.

During cooking stir vegetables several times to reposition them or to break up any frozen chunks.

Prick the skins of whole vegetables like jacket potatoes, tomatoes or aubergines to prevent their skins from bursting.

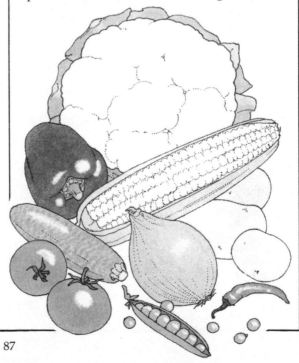

Cabbage with Smoked Sausage

TIMES		METHOD	SETTINGS	SERVINGS
PREP	COOK	MICRO. CONVEN.	HIGH	4
20	12			

450 g (1 lb) cabbage, thinly shredded

100 g (4 oz) butter or margarine

1 small onion, skinned and sliced

30 ml (2 level tbsp) plain flour

300 ml (½ pint) milk

15 ml (1 level tbsp) French mustard

salt and pepper

450 g (1 lb) smoked sausage, sliced

50 g (2 oz) fresh wholemeal breadcrumbs

15 ml (1 level tbsp) caraway seeds

1 Wash and drain the cabbage and place in a large casserole. Cover and microwave on HIGH for 5 minutes. Leave to stand, covered.

2 Place half the butter or margarine in a medium bowl and microwave on HIGH for 45 seconds or until melted. Stir in the onion and microwave on HIGH for 5–7 minutes or until soft.

3 Stir in the flour and microwave on HIGH for 30 seconds. Gradually whisk in the milk and microwave on HIGH for 4 minutes or until boiling and thickened, whisking once or twice to prevent lumps forming. Stir in the mustard and season to taste.

4 Drain the cabbage and return to the casserole. Pour over the sauce and mix lightly together.

5 Add the sausage, mix well and microwave on HIGH for 5 minutes or until heated through.

6 Melt the remaining butter or margarine in a small frying pan and sauté the breadcrumbs until crisp. Stir in the caraway seeds and spoon on top of the dish.

This dish makes a good midweek family meal. Serve with jacket potatoes.

Cucumber with Onion and Tarragon

TIMES		METHOD	SETTINGS	SERVINGS
PREP	COOK	MICRO.	HIGH	4
10	3			

1 cucumber

salt and pepper

15 g (½ oz) butter or margarine

30 ml (2 tbsp) chopped fresh tarragon

1 bunch of spring onions, trimmed and sliced

fresh tarragon sprigs, to garnish

1 Using a sharp knife or a canelle knife, remove thin strips of skin evenly from all round the cucumber, to make a striped pattern. Quarter the cucumber lengthways and cut into 5 cm (2 inch) chunks. Place in a colander and sprinkle liberally with salt. Leave for 20 minutes, then drain and pat dry with absorbent kitchen paper.

2 Put the cucumber, butter or margarine and tarragon into a large bowl and three-quarters cover with cling film. Microwave on HIGH for 1 minute, then add the spring onions and microwave on HIGH for 2 minutes or until the vegetables are tender. Garnish with fresh tarragon.

Serve hot with lamb chops and other lamb dishes.

COOK'S TIP

If you do not have fresh tarragon, use either fresh parsley or mint.

It is necessary to salt the cucumber to extract excess liquid. If you do not do this the sauce will be watery after cooking.

Green Beans with Coconut

TIMES		METHOD	SETTINGS	SERVINGS
PREP. **15**	COOK **22**	MICRO.	HIGH	4

50 g (2 oz) butter or margarine

1 large onion, skinned and finely chopped

50 g (2 oz) desiccated coconut

30 ml (2 tbsp) chopped fresh parsley

salt and pepper

450 g (1 lb) green beans, trimmed

1 Place the butter or margarine, onion and coconut in a shallow serving dish. Microwave on HIGH for 5–6 minutes or until the coconut turns a light golden colour. Stir once during the cooking time to coat the coconut with the fat. Stir in the parsley and seasoning and set aside.

2 Cut the beans into 5 cm (2 inch) lengths and place them in a medium bowl. Add 75 ml (5 tbsp) water. Three-quarters cover with cling film and microwave on HIGH for 12–14 minutes or until tender, stirring once. Drain the beans.

3 Reheat the coconut mixture on HIGH for 2 minutes, then add the cooked beans. Toss together and serve.

Serve with grilled or roast chicken or pork.

Advance preparation: the coconut mixture can be prepared in advance and stored covered in the refrigerator for up to 5 days.

COOK'S TIP

The crunchy coconut mixture can be used with other vegetables such as broccoli and cauliflower florets, mange-tout and peas. Cook the vegetables as directed on the chart (see pages 26–27).

Stuffed Aubergines

TIMES		METHOD	SETTINGS	SERVINGS
PREP. **15**	COOK **15**	MICRO. CONVEN.	HIGH	4

2 medium aubergines

30 ml (2 tbsp) olive oil

15 ml (1 tbsp) chopped fresh parsley

15 ml (1 tbsp) snipped chives

1 garlic clove, skinned and crushed

175 g (6 oz) button mushrooms, wiped and chopped

1 green pepper, seeded and chopped

salt and pepper

50 g (2 oz) fresh breadcrumbs

15 g (½ oz) walnuts, finely chopped

25 g (1 oz) Cheddar cheese, grated

1 Cut the aubergines in half lengthways. Scoop out the insides and coarsely chop the flesh. Reserve the shells.

2 In a medium bowl, combine the chopped aubergine with 15 ml (1 tbsp) oil, the herbs, garlic, mushrooms and green pepper. Season to taste. Microwave on HIGH for 6–7 minutes or until slightly softened, stirring occasionally.

3 Spoon the aubergine mixture into the reserved shells and level the surface. Place in a flameproof dish, brush all over with the remaining oil and cover. Microwave on HIGH for 6–8 minutes or until the aubergines are tender.

4 Mix the breadcrumbs, walnuts and cheese together and sprinkle over the aubergines. Place under a hot grill until browned on top.

Serve as a vegetarian lunch dish with a green salad and wholemeal rolls.

Minted Carrots and Brussels Sprouts

TIMES		METHOD	SETTINGS	SERVINGS
PREP	COOK			
15	14	MICRO.	HIGH	4

450 g (1 lb) brussels sprouts, trimmed

225 g (8 oz) carrots, peeled and sliced

50 g (2 oz) butter or margarine

30 ml (2 tbsp) chopped fresh mint

salt and pepper

1 Put the sprouts and carrots in a large casserole. Add 45 ml (3 tbsp) water and three-quarters cover with cling film. Microwave on HIGH for 9–12 minutes or until tender. Shake the casserole once during the cooking time.

2 Drain the vegetables and return to the casserole.

3 Place the butter or margarine and mint in a small measuring jug and microwave on HIGH for 1 minute or until melted and foaming. Pour the butter over the vegetables and toss until well coated.

4 Microwave on HIGH for 1 minute to reheat if necessary. Season to taste with salt and pepper and serve.

Serve as an accompaniment to poultry dishes.

Fennel with Mozzarella Cheese

TIMES		METHOD	SETTINGS	SERVINGS
PREP	COOK			
10	12	MICRO. CONVEN.	HIGH	4

2 large or 3 small fennel bulbs, total weight about 450 g (1 lb), trimmed

30 ml (2 tbsp) lemon juice

5 ml (1 tsp) fresh marjoram

1 bay leaf

salt and pepper

200 g (7 oz) mozzarella cheese, thinly sliced

1 Cut the fennel across into 0.5 cm (¼ inch) slices, reserving the feathery leaves.

2 Place the fennel in a shallow flameproof dish with the lemon juice, marjoram, bay leaf and 75 ml (5 tbsp) water. Three-quarters cover with cling film and microwave on HIGH for 9–10 minutes or until the fennel is tender. Stir occasionally during cooking.

3 Drain, discarding the bay leaf, and return the vegetable to the dish. Season to taste and lay the cheese over the fennel. Grill under a hot grill until the cheese is golden brown and bubbling. Serve immediately, garnished with the reserved leaves.

Serve with roast or grilled veal.

COOK'S TIP

For best flavour, choose the Italian mozzarella cheese sold in bags at delicatessens. Otherwise, the Danish or Scottish mozzarella may be used.

Stuffed Onions

TIMES PREP 30 | COOK 23	METHOD MICRO.	SETTINGS HIGH	SERVINGS 4

4 large Spanish onions, each weighing about 225 g (8 oz), skinned and trimmed

1 garlic clove, skinned and crushed

15 g (½ oz) butter or margarine

50 g (2 oz) fresh brown breadcrumbs

1.25 ml (¼ level tsp) ground cumin

1.25 ml (¼ level tsp) ground coriander

pinch of chilli powder

salt and pepper

40 g (1½ oz) pine nuts, chopped

40 g (1½ oz) sultanas

30 ml (2 tbsp) chopped fresh parsley

5 ml (1 tsp) lemon juice

1 Cut a slice from the top of each onion and remove the centre, leaving a shell about 0.5 cm (¼ inch) thick.

2 Finely chop 100 g (4 oz) of the scooped-out onion and place in a small bowl with the garlic, butter or margarine, breadcrumbs and spices. Season to taste with salt and pepper and mix well.

3 Three-quarters cover with cling film and microwave on HIGH for 3 minutes or until the onion is beginning to soften, stirring once.

4 Add the nuts, sultanas, 15 ml (1 tbsp) chopped parsley and the lemon juice. Mix well and spoon into the onion shells.

5 Place the stuffed onions in a shallow dish, cover and microwave on HIGH for 15 minutes. Turn the dish twice during cooking. Leave to stand, covered for 5 minutes. Sprinkle with the remaining parsley.

Serve hot with fresh tomato sauce (see page 114)

Stuffed Peppers

TIMES PREP 20 | COOK 26	METHOD MICRO.	SETTINGS LOW HIGH	SERVINGS 4

4 green or red peppers

For the filling:

1 small onion, skinned and chopped

1 garlic clove, skinned and chopped

15 ml (1 tbsp) vegetable oil

2.5 ml (½ level tsp) ground coriander

2.5 ml (½ level tsp) ground cumin

2.5 ml (½ level tsp) garam masala

2.5 ml (½ level tsp) ground ginger

1 chicken breast, skinned, boned and cut into small pieces

225 g (8 oz) cooked long grain rice

25 g (1 oz) almonds, roughly chopped

25 g (1 oz) currants

salt and pepper

142 g (5 oz) natural yogurt

1 Cut a slice from the tops of the peppers and remove the cores and seeds. Stand in a small dish, with the slice cut from the tops, and add 60 ml (4 tbsp) water. Cover and microwave on HIGH for 6 minutes; quarter turn the dish three times during cooking. Leave to stand while making the filling.

2 Mix the onion, garlic, oil and spices together in a large bowl and microwave on HIGH for 5 minutes, stirring occasionally.

3 Add the chicken and microwave on HIGH for 5 minutes, or until the chicken is cooked, stirring occasionally.

4 Stir in the rice, almonds and currants and season to taste. Add the yogurt and mix well.

5 Stuff the peppers with the filling and replace the lids. Cover and microwave on LOW for 10 minutes or until the peppers are cooked and the filling reheated; quarter turn the dish three times during cooking. Serve hot.

Chinese Fried Vegetables

TIMES		METHOD	SETTINGS	SERVINGS
PREP	COOK	MICRO.	HIGH	4
10	5			

2.5 cm (1 inch) piece fresh root ginger

30 ml (2 tbsp) vegetable oil

50 g (2 oz) mange-tout, trimmed

50 g (2 oz) mushrooms, wiped and sliced

75 g (3 oz) beansprouts

227 g (8 oz) can sliced bamboo shoots, drained

50 g (2 oz) cashew nuts

15 ml (1 tbsp) soy sauce

pepper

1 Peel the ginger and thinly slice. Place in a large shallow dish along with the oil. Microwave on HIGH for 1 minute to heat the oil.

2 Stir in the mange-tout, mushrooms and beansprouts. Microwave on HIGH for 2 minutes, stirring once.

3 Add the bamboo shoots, cashew nuts and soy sauce. Microwave on HIGH for 2 minutes or until hot. Season with pepper and serve.

For a vegetarian main course, serve with boiled rice. This dish is also good served with roast chicken.

COOK'S TIP

For a slimmers' vegetable dish, omit the oil and use 15 ml (1 tbsp) water instead.

Spinach and Potato Bake

TIMES		METHOD	SETTINGS	SERVINGS
PREP	COOK	MICRO. CONVEN.	HIGH	4
25	25			

700 g (1½ lb) potatoes, peeled and thinly sliced

25 g (1 oz) butter or margarine

60 ml (4 tbsp) double cream

pinch of grated nutmeg

salt and pepper

450 g (1 lb) fresh spinach, washed, trimmed and finely chopped

45 ml (3 level tbsp) fresh breadcrumbs

45 ml (3 level tbsp) grated Parmesan cheese

1 Place the potatoes and half the butter or margarine in a shallow flameproof dish. Microwave on HIGH for 5 minutes, stirring twice.

2 Stir in the cream, nutmeg and seasoning. Spread the spinach evenly over the top of the potatoes.

3 Cover and microwave on HIGH for 12 minutes or until the potatoes are tender. Give the dish a half-turn once during cooking. Leave to stand for 5 minutes.

4 Mix the breadcrumbs and cheese together and sprinkle the mixture over the spinach. Dot with the remaining butter or margarine. Brown under a hot grill.

Serve with lamb dishes.

COOK'S TIP

Use 225 g (8 oz) frozen spinach, thawed and thoroughly drained, instead of fresh spinach.

Leeks in Tomato and Basil Sauce

TIMES		METHOD	SETTINGS	SERVINGS
PREP	COOK	MICRO.	HIGH	4
20	20			

30 ml (2 tbsp) olive oil

1 garlic clove, skinned and crushed

450 g (1 lb) marmande or beef tomatoes, skinned and coarsely chopped

15 ml (1 level tbsp) soft dark brown sugar

30 ml (2 tbsp) chopped fresh basil

salt and pepper

450 g (1 lb) leeks, trimmed, thickly sliced and washed

fresh basil, to garnish

1 Place the oil and garlic in a large bowl and microwave on HIGH for 2 minutes. Add the tomatoes, sugar, chopped basil and seasoning.

2 Three-quarters cover with cling film and microwave on HIGH for 10 minutes or until the sauce has thickened, stirring twice.

3 Add the leeks and stir well. Microwave on HIGH for 8 minutes or until the leeks are tender. Garnish with basil leaves and serve.

For a vegetarian lunch, serve with crusty bread and grated Parmesan cheese.

Cauliflower with Lemon

TIMES		METHOD	SETTINGS	SERVINGS
PREP	COOK	MICRO.	HIGH	4
7	10			

700 g (1½ lb) cauliflower, trimmed

30 ml (2 tbsp) lemon juice

paprika, to garnish

1 Divide the cauliflower into small florets, discarding the stalks.

2 Place the florets in a shallow dish and pour over the lemon juice. Three-quarters cover with cling film and microwave on HIGH for 10 minutes.

3 Sprinkle with paprika and serve.

Serve the cauliflower with ham, bacon or pork.

COOK'S TIP

Cauliflower is rather difficult to cook evenly in the microwave due to the difference in texture of the florets and stalk. It is therefore best to divide into florets for even cooking and use the stalks for making soups.

Cabbage with Soured Cream and Caraway

TIMES		METHOD	SETTINGS	SERVINGS
PREP.	COOK			
10	9	MICRO.	HIGH	4

700 g (1½ lb) cabbage

25 g (1 oz) butter or margarine

10 ml (2 level tsp) caraway seeds

142 ml (5 fl oz) soured cream

salt and pepper

1 Finely shred the cabbage, discarding any tough stalk.

2 Place the butter or margarine in a medium casserole and microwave on HIGH for 45 seconds or until melted. Add the cabbage and the caraway seeds and mix together well.

3 Three-quarters cover with cling flim and microwave on HIGH for 7 minutes, stirring twice.

4 Stir in the soured cream and microwave on HIGH for 1 minute. Season and serve hot.

Serve as an accompaniment to game and pork dishes.

Advance preparation: The dish can be prepared in advance to the end of Stage 3. Cover and refrigerate until ready to serve, then reheat and continue with Stage 4.

> **COOK'S TIP**
>
> Do not allow the soured cream to boil or it will separate.

Glazed Vegetables Provençal

TIMES		METHOD	SETTINGS	SERVINGS
PREP.	COOK			
15	4	MICRO.	HIGH	4

25 g (1 oz) butter or margarine

1 garlic clove, skinned and crushed

half a red pepper, seeded and cut into strips

half a yellow pepper, seeded and cut into strips

half a green pepper, seeded and cut into strips

1 courgette, thinly sliced

50 g (2 oz) mange-tout, trimmed

1 large tomato, skinned, seeded and cut into strips

60 ml (4 tbsp) dry white wine

salt and pepper

fresh basil, to garnish

1 Preheat a browning dish according to the manufacturer's instructions. Add the butter or margarine and garlic for the last 30 seconds of heating.

2 Add the vegetables and stir. Microwave on HIGH for 2–3 minutes or until the vegetables are slightly softened.

3 Stir in the white wine and season to taste with salt and pepper. Microwave on HIGH for 1 minute. Garnish with fresh basil and serve.

Serve with chicken or turkey or for a vegetarian meal, serve with brown rice.

> **COOK'S TIP**
>
> This dish can be prepared without a browning dish; place the butter or margarine and garlic in a large shallow dish and microwave for 1 minute, then add the vegetables and continue as above.

Broccoli with Almonds and Garlic

TIMES		METHOD	SETTINGS	SERVINGS
PREP.	COOK	MICRO.	HIGH	4
8	9			

700 g (1½ lb) broccoli

30 ml (2 tbsp) vegetable oil

2 garlic cloves, skinned and crushed

25 g (1 oz) flaked almonds

salt and pepper

1 Wash the broccoli and break into small even-sized florets, discarding any tough stalks.

2 Stir the oil, garlic and almonds together in a shallow dish large enough to hold the broccoli in a single layer. Microwave on HIGH for 2 minutes.

3 Add the broccoli and stir until coated in the oil. Three-quarters cover with cling film and microwave on HIGH for 7 minutes or until tender. Stir twice during the cooking time. Season to taste with salt and pepper and serve at once.

Serve with trout or grilled white fish steaks. It also makes an excellent accompaniment to beef.

Vegetable Curry

TIMES		METHOD	SETTINGS	SERVINGS
PREP.	COOK	MICRO.	HIGH	6
20	24			

450 g (1 lb) cauliflower, broken into florets

50 g (2 oz) butter or margarine

1 medium onion, skinned and chopped

15–30 ml (1–2 level tbsp) curry paste

30 ml (2 level tbsp) tomato purée

90 ml (6 level tbsp) plain flour

15 ml (1 level tbsp) granulated sugar

600 ml (1 pint) boiling chicken stock

450 g (1 lb) courgettes, trimmed and sliced

425 g (15 oz) can chick peas, drained

1 Place the cauliflower in a medium bowl with 45 ml (3 tbsp) water. Cover and microwave on HIGH for 3 minutes. Leave to stand, covered.

2 Place the butter or margarine in a large casserole and microwave on HIGH for 45 seconds or until melted. Add the onion and microwave on HIGH for 5–7 minutes or until softened.

3 Add the curry paste, tomato purée, flour and sugar and microwave on HIGH for 30 seconds. Gradually blend in the stock and microwave on HIGH for 3 minutes or until boiling and thickened, stirring once or twice.

4 Fold in the courgettes and drained cauliflower. Cover and microwave on HIGH for 8 minutes, stirring once. Add the chick peas and microwave on HIGH for 2 minutes.

Serve the vegetable curry with boiled rice as a main course.

COOK'S TIP

For a more substantial dish, add 3 hard-boiled eggs, quartered. Stir the eggs into the curry at the end of stage 4.

Sliced Potatoes with Mustard

TIMES		METHOD	SETTINGS	SERVINGS
PREP	COOK	MICRO.	HIGH	
15	26	CONVEN.		6

25 g (1 oz) butter or margarine

1 large onion, skinned and sliced

900 g (2 lb) potatoes, peeled and thinly sliced

150 ml (5 fl oz) single cream

15 ml (1 level tbsp) whole-grain mustard

salt and pepper

1 Place the butter or margarine in a shallow flameproof dish and microwave on HIGH for 45 seconds or until melted. Add the onion and microwave on HIGH for 3 minutes or until the onion begins to soften. Add the potato slices and toss to combine with the onion.

2 Whisk the cream and mustard together. Season to taste with salt and pepper and add to the potatoes. Three-quarters cover with cling film and microwave on HIGH for 15 minutes or until the potatoes are tender. Leave to stand for 5 minutes, then remove the cling film.

3 Brown under a hot grill, if desired, and serve hot.

This dish makes a tasty accompaniment to boiled or baked gammon.

COOK'S TIP

Take care when uncovering the dish at the end of Stage 5: starting at the edge furthest from you, peel the cling film towards you to avoid steam burns.

Carrots with Spring Onions and Orange

TIMES		METHOD	SETTINGS	SERVINGS
PREP	COOK	MICRO.	HIGH	
20	10			4

900 g (2 lb) carrots, peeled

1 bunch of spring onions, trimmed and sliced

25 g (1 oz) butter or margarine, cut into small pieces

60 ml (4 tbsp) orange juice

salt and pepper

10 ml (2 tsp) chopped fresh mint, to garnish

1 Cut the carrots into strips about 5 cm (2 inches) long and 0.5 cm (¼ inch) wide.

2 Place the carrots and spring onions in a shallow dish. Add the butter or margarine and the orange juice. Season to taste with salt and pepper.

3 Three-quarters cover with cling film and microwave on HIGH for 8–10 minutes or until tender but still firm. Check after 8 minutes and return to the oven for 1–2 minutes, if necessary. Garnish with mint.

Serve with roast lamb.

COOK'S TIP

If using small new carrots, cook them whole. Microwave on HIGH for 10–12 minutes or until tender.

Chocolate creams (Desserts) *opposite*

COOK

3:00

POWER
LEVEL   TIME   CLOCK

Chicory and Ham au Gratin

TIMES PREP. 10 / COOK 20	METHOD MICRO. CONVEN.	SETTINGS HIGH	SERVINGS 4

300 ml (½ pint) milk

1 small onion, skinned and quartered

1 small carrot, peeled and sliced

half a small celery stick, sliced

2 cloves

6 black peppercorns

1 blade mace

1 parsley sprig

1 thyme sprig

1 bay leaf

25 g (1 oz) butter or margarine

25 g (1 oz) plain flour

4 even-sized heads chicory

4 slices cooked ham

50 g (2 oz) Cheddar cheese, grated

1 Combine the milk, onion, carrot, celery, cloves, peppercorns, mace and herbs in a large bowl. Cover and microwave on HIGH for 5 minutes or until boiling. Set aside to infuse for 30 minutes. Strain and discard the vegetables, spices and herbs.

2 Place the butter or margarine in a medium bowl and microwave on HIGH for 45 seconds or until melted. Stir in the flour and microwave on HIGH for 30 seconds. Gradually whisk in the milk and microwave on HIGH for 2–3 minutes, whisking every 30 seconds, until thickened.

3 In a shallow flameproof dish, arrange the chicory in a single layer, add 60 ml (4 tbsp) water, cover and microwave on HIGH for 5–8 minutes or until tender. Drain well.

4 Wrap each head of chicory in a slice of ham and place in the dish seam side down. Pour over the sauce and microwave on HIGH for 1 minute or until hot.

5 Sprinkle with the cheese and grill under a hot grill until the cheese is golden.

Serve with green salad.

Creamed Mushrooms with Cumin

TIMES PREP. 10 / COOK 7	METHOD MICRO.	SETTINGS HIGH	SERVINGS 4

25 g (1 oz) butter or margarine

450 g (1 lb) mushrooms, wiped and sliced

5 ml (1 level tsp) ground cumin

30 ml (2 level tbsp) plain flour

200 ml (7 fl oz) milk

salt and pepper

chopped fresh parsley, to garnish

1 Place the butter or margarine in a medium bowl and microwave on HIGH for 45 seconds or until melted. Add the mushrooms and cumin and stir to coat in the fat. Three-quarters cover with cling film and microwave on HIGH for 2 minutes.

2 Stir in the flour and microwave on HIGH for 30 seconds. Gradually add the milk and season to taste with salt and pepper. Microwave on HIGH for 4 minutes or until the sauce thickens, whisking after every minute. Serve, garnished with chopped parsley.

Serve as an accompaniment to roast or grilled pork. The creamed mushrooms can also be served on hot buttered toast to make a tasty snack.

COOK'S TIP

Mushrooms should not be washed as they absorb water and lose their delicate flavour and firm texture. Instead gently wipe them with a clean damp cloth. Only peel large mushrooms if necessary because much of the flavour is contained in the skin.

Apricot flapjacks (Baking) *opposite*

Desserts

Most desserts cook superbly in the microwave, especially steamed puddings which become moist and light in about 10 minutes. Puddings need only be lightly covered with cling film, pressed close to the sides of the basin and tented in the centre to allow room for the pudding to rise. A pudding cooks in its own moisture – no water needs to be added.

However, steamed fruit puddings should be stored in the freezer, unlike conventionally made fruit puddings. This is because with microwaved steamed fruit puddings mould develops within a few weeks of making. Wrap the pudding in foil, overwrap and store in the freezer for up to 12 months.

The microwave can be an enormous help with the many small tasks necessary for making desserts. Eggs stored in the refrigerator can be microwaved on HIGH for 3 seconds to take the chill off them, which helps them whisk to a greater volume; take care though as eggs may burst if microwaved for longer.

Instead of toasting, almonds can be microwaved on HIGH for 8–10 minutes for a golden brown finish – no need to preheat the grill or oven. To skin hazel nuts, microwave on HIGH for 30 seconds then rub in a tea towel to remove the skins. Give desiccated coconut a lovely brown colour by microwaving it in a roasting bag for 5 minutes on HIGH.

Fruit

Fruits retain their colours and flavours when microwaved. Most fruits need only a little water added in which to cook so that flavours are never diluted. Rhubarb and cooking apples and other fruits high in water can be microwaved without added water. Red currants and black currants should be cooked in enough water to cover them as this helps to soften their tough skins; other berry fruits such as raspberries require no additional water.

Whole fruits should be pierced to prevent them from bursting.

Cook fruit and fruit fillings in the microwave and use for making desserts in the conventional way. Cook pastry conventionally then fill it with the fruit filling.

Dried Fruit

Dried fruits make simple yet delicious winter fruit salads and compotes and there is no need for lengthy overnight soaking to soften the fruit when the microwave is used. Dried fruits can be cooked with just enough water for them to absorb. For every 225 g (8 oz) apricots, peaches or pears or a mixture of these fruits, cover with 600 ml (1 pint) water and microwave on HIGH for 10 minutes. Leave to stand for 10 minutes. Cook 450 g (1 lb) prunes in 600 ml (1 pint) water or tea for 15 minutes and leave to stand for 15 minutes. Whole figs should be first soaked for about 2 hours and then microwaved without added water for 10 minutes. Sweeten the fruit before cooking.

Brandied Apricot Trifle

TIMES		METHOD	SETTINGS	SERVINGS
PREP.	COOK	MICRO.	LOW	
20	19		HIGH	6

225 g (8 oz) jam-filled Swiss roll, sliced

439 g (14½ oz) can apricots, drained

60 ml (4 tbsp) brandy

568 ml (1 pint) milk

6 eggs

90 ml (6 level tbsp) granulated sugar

300 ml (10 fl oz) whipping cream

25 g (1 oz) flaked almonds, toasted

1 Line the base and sides of a 1.4 litre (2½ pint) glass dish with the slices of Swiss roll.

2 Arrange the apricots over the sponge, reserving a few for decoration, and sprinkle with the brandy.

3 Pour the milk into a medium bowl and microwave on HIGH for 4 minutes or until scalded. Beat in the eggs and sugar, then strain the custard over the fruit.

4 Cover with cling film and microwave on LOW for 15 minutes or until the custard is set around the edges but still liquid in the centre. Leave to cool, then cover and chill overnight.

5 Whip the cream until stiff and pipe or spoon it on the trifle. Decorate with the reserved apricots and the almonds.

Old English Eggnog Pie

TIMES		METHOD	SETTINGS	SERVINGS
PREP.	COOK	MICRO.	MEDIUM	
25	40	CONVEN.	HIGH	6

175 g (6 oz) plain flour

pinch of salt

125 g (4 oz) butter or margarine

45 ml (3 level tbsp) ground almonds

90 ml (6 level tbsp) caster sugar

3 egg yolks

15 ml (1 level tbsp) powdered gelatine

45 ml (3 tbsp) rum

410 g (14½ oz) can evaporated milk

5 ml (1 level tsp) grated nutmeg

150 ml (5 fl oz) double cream

1 egg white

chocolate curls, to decorate

1 Place the flour and salt in a bowl. Cut the fat into pieces and rub into the flour until the mixture resembles fine breadcrumbs. Stir in the almonds and half the sugar. Mix to a soft dough with 1 egg yolk and 15 ml (1 tbsp) water.

2 Roll out the dough on a lightly floured surface and use to line a 23 cm (9 inch) deep loose-bottomed flat tin. Chill for 20–30 minutes.

3 Bake blind at 200°C (400°F) mark 6 for 15 minutes until set. Remove the baking beans and bake for 10–12 minutes until golden. Remove from tin and cool.

4 In a small bowl, sprinkle the gelatine over the rum and leave to soften. Pour the milk into a small bowl and microwave on HIGH for 3 minutes.

5 Whisk the remaining egg yolks and sugar in a large bowl until pale and creamy. Gradually whisk in the hot milk and add the nutmeg. Microwave on MEDIUM for 8–9 minutes, stirring frequently, until starting to thicken. Stir in the gelatine and leave to cool.

6 Whip the cream. Whisk the egg white until stiff. Fold into the custard, then spoon into the flan case. Chill until set, then decorate.

Fruit Brûlée

TIMES PREP | COOK	METHOD	SETTINGS	SERVINGS
15 | 30	MICRO. CONVEN.	LOW HIGH	6

568 ml (1 pint) milk

4 eggs, size 2

75 ml (5 level tbsp) caster sugar

225 g (8 oz) fresh raspberries or sliced strawberries

150 ml (5 fl oz) double cream

142 g (5 oz) natural yogurt

60 ml (4 level tbsp) soft brown sugar

1 Pour the milk into a large bowl and microwave on HIGH for 4 minutes or until hot, but not boiling. Beat in the eggs and 15 ml (1 level tbsp) caster sugar. Strain into a 750 ml (1¼ pint) straight-sided flameproof dish.

2 Cover with cling film and place the dish in a larger dish with a capacity of about 1.7 litres (3 pints). Pour in enough boiling water to come halfway up the sides of the dish.

3 Microwave on LOW for 18–20 minutes, or until lightly set. Quarter turn the dish three times during cooking.

4 Leave to stand for 5 minutes, then remove the dish from the water, uncover and leave to cool. Re-cover and chill overnight.

5 Arrange the fruit on top of the custard. Lightly whip the cream and yogurt together and spoon it over the fruit.

6 Mix the remaining castor sugar with the brown sugar and spread evenly over the cream. Place under a hot grill and grill until the sugar melts and turns golden brown. Chill before serving. To serve, tap gently with a spoon to break the caramel.

Spiced Plum Sponge

TIMES PREP | COOK	METHOD	SETTINGS	SERVINGS
10 | 8	MICRO.	HIGH	4

75 g (3 oz) butter or margarine

75 g (3 oz) soft light brown sugar

2 eggs

100 g (4 oz) self-raising flour

2.5 ml (½ level tsp) ground cinnamon

425 g (15 oz) can plums

1 Cream the butter or margarine and sugar together until light and fluffy. Gradually beat in the eggs and then fold in the flour and cinnamon.

2 Drain and stone the plums, discarding the juice. Arrange the fruit in the base of an 18 cm (7 inch) soufflé dish and cover with the sponge mixture.

3 Microwave on HIGH for 8 minutes or until the sponge is firm to the touch.

Serve hot with custard.

COOK'S TIP

To soften brown sugar which has become hard and lumpy, microwave it on HIGH for 40–50 seconds in the original wrapping.

Chilled Orange Soufflé

TIMES		METHOD	SETTINGS	SERVINGS
PREP.	COOK			
25	6	MICRO.	HIGH	6

15 ml (1 level tbsp) powdered gelatine

178 ml (6¼ oz) carton frozen concentrated orange juice, thawed

100 g (4 oz) granulated sugar

pinch of salt

3 eggs, separated

300 ml (10 fl oz) double cream

1 orange, segmented

1 Tie a collar of greaseproof paper around a 15 cm (6 inch) soufflé dish to extend 7.5 cm (3 inches) above the dish.

2 Sprinkle the gelatine over the orange juice in a large bowl and leave to soften.

3 Beat half the sugar, the salt and egg yolks into the orange and gelatine mixture. Microwave on HIGH for 6 minutes, stirring after every minute, until thick and smooth. Do not allow to boil. Leave to cool.

4 Whisk the egg whites until stiff, then gradually whisk in the remaining sugar.

5 Lightly whip the cream. Fold first the cream then the egg whites into the orange custard and pour into the prepared dish. Leave to set in the refrigerator for at least 3 hours. Remove the paper collar, decorate with the orange segments and serve.

Apricot and Cheese Crêpes

TIMES		METHOD	SETTINGS	SERVINGS
PREP.	COOK			
10	3	MICRO.	HIGH	4

8 pancakes (see page 49)

For the filling:

90 ml (6 level tbsp) apricot jam

100 g (4 oz) full-fat soft cheese

50 g (2 oz) sultanas

25 g (1 oz) butter or margarine

60 ml (4 tbsp) brandy, preferably apricot brandy

1 To make the filling, beat together the jam and cheese and fold in the sultanas.

2 Divide the mixture between the pancakes and spread to within 1 cm (½ inch) of the edges. Fold the pancakes in half and in half again to form triangles.

3 Place the butter or margarine in a flan dish and microwave on HIGH for 45 seconds or until melted. Arrange the filled pancakes in the dish with the pointed ends towards the centre. Microwave on HIGH for 2 minutes.

4 Place the brandy in a small jug or cup and microwave on HIGH for 30 seconds. Pour the hot brandy over the crêpes and set alight. Serve immediately.

COOK'S TIP

To plump sultanas or raisins, cover with water and microwave on HIGH for 5 minutes. Stir, leave to stand, then drain and dry with absorbent kitchen paper before using.

Zabaglione

TIMES		METHOD	SETTINGS	SERVINGS
PREP	COOK			
15	3	MICRO.	HIGH	4

4 egg yolks

50 g (2 oz) caster sugar

100 ml (4 fl oz) Marsala

1 In a medium bowl, beat the egg yolks and sugar together until pale and creamy.

2 Stir in the Marsala and microwave on HIGH for 2½-3 minutes, whisking several times.

3 When the mixture starts to thicken around the edges, beat with a hand-held electric mixer for about 5 minutes until smooth and thick. Spoon into four small glasses and leave to cool.

Serve at room temperature with small crisp biscuits.

Variations
Zabaglione Cream: at the end of stage 3, continue beating and gradually add 150 ml (5 fl oz) whipping cream.

Iced Zabaglione: spoon the mixture into a freezer-proof container, cover and freeze for at least 6 hours until frozen. To serve, thaw in the microwave on MEDIUM for 30–45 seconds, then leave to stand for 1 minute until slightly softened.

Chilled Lemon Cream

TIMES		METHOD	SETTINGS	SERVINGS
PREP	COOK			
30	5	MICRO.	HIGH	6

45 ml (3 level tbsp) cornflour

finely grated rind and juice of 2 lemons

75 g (3 oz) caster sugar

3 eggs, separated

150 ml (5 fl oz) double cream

lemon twists and angelica, to decorate

1 Mix the cornflour, lemon rind, lemon juice, sugar and 150 ml (¼ pint) water together in a medium bowl.

2 Microwave on HIGH for 4 minutes, stirring two or three times, until thick and smooth, then beat in the egg yolks. Microwave on HIGH for 45 seconds, whisking once. Cover and leave to cool.

3 Whip the cream until stiff and whisk the egg whites until stiff. Fold first the cream then the egg whites into the lemon mixture.

4 Spoon into individual serving glasses and chill. Decorate with lemon twists and angelica and serve.

COOK'S TIP

When the lemon cream is cooling at the end of stage 2, lay cling film or damp greaseproof paper on the surface to prevent a skin from forming.

Macaroon Flan

TIMES PREP.	COOK	METHOD	SETTINGS	SERVINGS
20	10	MICRO. CONVEN.	HIGH	6

23 cm (9 inch) flan case (see page 105)

15 g (½ oz) icing sugar

angelica and glacé cherries, to decorate

For the filling:

700 g (1½ lb) cooking apples, peeled and grated

60 ml (4 level tbsp) mincemeat

3 egg whites

100 g (4 oz) ground almonds

75 g (3 oz) caster sugar

1 Mix the apples and mincemeat together and spoon into the flan case. Microwave on HIGH for 7–8 minutes or until the apple is cooked.

2 Whisk the egg whites until stiff and fold in the almonds and caster sugar.

3 Spoon into a piping bag fitted with a large star nozzle and pipe on top of the flan.

4 Place under a hot grill until golden brown. Dust with icing sugar and decorate with glacé cherries and angelica. Serve the flan warm.

COOK'S TIP

This flan tastes best when served warm, but do not reheat it once it has been topped with the meringue. If liked, make the filling in advance and just before serving make the topping and place the flan under the hot grill.

Chocolate Creams

TIMES PREP.	COOK	METHOD	SETTINGS	SERVINGS
20	8	MICRO.	MEDIUM HIGH	8

15 ml (1 level tbsp) powdered gelatine

30 ml (2 tbsp) rum or strong coffee

100 g (4 oz) plain dessert chocolate

3 eggs, separated

pinch of salt

410 g (14½ oz) can evaporated milk

100 g (4 oz) granulated sugar

300 ml (10 fl oz) double cream

chocolate curls or rice paper flowers, to decorate

1 Sprinkle the gelatine over the rum or coffee in a small bowl and leave to soften.

2 Break the chocolate into a large bowl and microwave on HIGH for 2 minutes or until melted. Beat in the gelatine with rum or coffee, egg yolks, salt, evaporated milk and 50 g (2 oz) sugar.

3 Microwave on MEDIUM for 6 minutes or until thickened and smooth, stirring several times. Leave to stand at room temperature until cool (do not refrigerate).

4 Lightly whip the cream and fold half into the chocolate mixture.

5 Whisk the egg whites until stiff and fold in the remaining sugar. Gently fold into the chocolate cream.

6 Spoon into individual serving glasses and chill. Pipe the remaining cream on top of the chocolate creams. Decorate each dish with chocolate curls or rice paper flowers and serve.

Saucy Chocolate Pudding

 TIMES PREP 10 COOK 14
 METHOD MICRO.
 SETTINGS HIGH
 SERVINGS 4

100 g (4 oz) plain flour
75 ml (5 level tbsp) cocoa
10 ml (2 level tsp) baking powder
pinch of salt
275 g (10 oz) soft light brown sugar
175 ml (6 fl oz) milk
30 ml (2 tbsp) vegetable oil
5 ml (1 tsp) vanilla flavouring
50 g (2 oz) walnuts, finely chopped

1 Sift the flour, 10 ml (2 level tbsp) cocoa, baking powder and salt into a large bowl. Stir in 100 g (4 oz) sugar.

2 Make a well in the centre and pour in the milk, oil and vanilla flavouring. Beat to a smooth batter. Stir in the nuts.

3 Pour the mixture into a 20.5 cm (8 inch) baking dish. Mix the remaining sugar and cocoa together and sprinkle evenly over the batter.

4 Pour over 350 ml (12 fl oz) boiling water. Microwave on HIGH for 12–14 minutes or until the top looks dry and the sauce is bubbling through.

Caribbean Bananas

 TIMES PREP 10 COOK 6
METHOD MICRO.
SETTINGS HIGH
 SERVINGS 4

25 g (1 oz) butter or margarine
50 g (2 oz) soft dark brown sugar
4 large bananas, peeled and halved
60 ml (4 tbsp) dark rum

1 Place the butter or margarine in a shallow dish and microwave on HIGH for 45 seconds or until melted. Add the sugar and microwave on HIGH for 1 minute. Stir until the sugar has dissolved.

2 Add the bananas and coat with the sugar mixture. Microwave on HIGH for 4 minutes, turning the fruit over once.

3 Place the rum in a cup and microwave on HIGH for 30 seconds, pour over the bananas and flambé immediately. Serve at once.

Serve with cream.

COOK'S TIP

It is safer to use a lighted taper rather than a match when igniting the rum.

Flan Case

TIMES		METHOD	MAKES
PREP	COOK	CONVEN.	23 cm (9 inch)
7	27		

225 g (8 oz) plain flour

pinch of salt

50 g (2 oz) butter or margarine

50 g (2 oz) lard

1 Place the flour and salt in a bowl. Cut the fats into small pieces and add to the flour. Rub the fat into the flour until the mixture resembles fine breadcrumbs. Add enough water to bind the mixture together.

2 Knead lightly for a few seconds to make a firm smooth dough.

3 Roll out the dough on a lightly floured surface and use to line a 23 cm (9 inch) flan ring set on a baking sheet. Chill in the refrigerator for 20–30 minutes.

4 Bake blind conventionally at 200°C (400°F) mark 6 for 15 minutes until set. Remove the baking beans and bake for a further 10–12 minutes until golden brown. Remove from the tin and leave on a wire rack until cool.

To make enough pastry to line a 20.5 cm (8 inch) flan case: use 175 g (6 oz) plain flour and 40 g (1½ oz) butter or margarine and 40 g (1½ oz) lard.

Walnut Pie

TIMES		METHOD	SETTINGS	SERVINGS
PREP	COOK	MICRO.	MEDIUM	8
5	19		HIGH	

23 cm (9 inch) flan case (see above)

whipped cream, to serve

For the filling:

50 g (2 oz) butter or margarine

3 eggs

175 g (6 oz) soft dark brown sugar

75 ml (5 tbsp) golden syrup

5 ml (1 tsp) vanilla flavouring

175 g (6 oz) walnuts, coarsely chopped

1 Place the butter or margarine in a medium bowl and microwave on HIGH for 45 seconds or until melted.

2 Beat in the eggs, sugar, syrup and flavouring, then stir in the nuts.

3 Pour into the flan case and microwave on MEDIUM for 18 minutes or until set. Leave to cool, and serve at room temperature with whipped cream.

COOK'S TIP

The texture of golden syrup or honey that has crystallised can be restored by microwaving on HIGH for 1–2 minutes. Always remove metal lids and if necessary transfer the syrup or honey to a glass jar.

Lemon Meringue Pie

TIMES		METHOD	SETTINGS	SERVINGS
PREP	COOK	MICRO.	HIGH	6
15	7	CONVEN.		

20.5 cm (8 inch) flan case (see page 105)

For the filling:

45 ml (3 level tbsp) cornflour

finely grated rind and juice of 2 lemons

200 g (7 oz) caster sugar

3 eggs, separated

1 Pour 150 ml (¼ pint) water into a medium bowl and mix in the cornflour, lemon rind, lemon juice and 75 g (3 oz) sugar. Microwave on HIGH for 4–5 minutes or until smooth and thick, stirring several times.

2 Beat in the egg yolks and microwave on HIGH for 45 seconds, whisking once. Pour the mixture into the baked flan case.

3 Whisk the egg whites until stiff and gradually fold in the remaining sugar. Spoon or pipe the whisked whites on top of the lemon filling.

4 Place the pie under a hot grill until the topping is golden brown on top.

Curd Cheese Flan

TIMES		METHOD	SETTINGS	SERVINGS
PREP	COOK	MICRO.	LOW	8
25	22		HIGH	

50 g (2 oz) butter or margarine

75 g (3 oz) digestive biscuits, crushed

450 g (1 lb) curd cheese

3 eggs

100 g (4 oz) demerara sugar

finely grated rind of 1 lemon

50 g (2 oz) sultanas

142 ml (5 fl oz) soured cream

pinch of grated nutmeg

1 Place the butter or margarine in a bowl and microwave on HIGH for 45 seconds or until melted.

2 Pour half the fat into a blender or food processor and set aside. Mix the fat remaining in the bowl with the crushed biscuits. Reserve 45 ml (3 tbsp) crumbs and press the rest on to the base of a 23 cm (9 inch) flan dish. Microwave on HIGH for 1 minute.

3 Add the cheese, eggs, sugar and lemon rind to the blender or food processor and blend until smooth. Stir in the sultanas and pour into the flan dish. Microwave on LOW for 20 minutes or until set around the edges. Leave to stand at room temperature for 1 hour.

4 Spread the soured cream evenly over the top of the flan. Mix the nutmeg with the reserved crumb mixture and sprinkle it over the top of the flan. Serve at room temperature.

COOK'S TIP

After microwaving for 20 minutes, the cheese filling will be set around the edges and soft in the centre. During standing the centre will set.

Butterscotch Apples

TIMES		METHOD	SETTINGS	SERVINGS
PREP	**COOK**	MICRO.	HIGH	4
10	8			

4 large eating apples

25 g (1 oz) walnuts, finely chopped

25 g (1 oz) sultanas

60 ml (4 tbsp) golden syrup

30 ml (2 tbsp) lemon juice

1 Core the apples and slit the skins around the centres. Fill each apple with the walnuts and sultanas.

2 Place the golden syrup, lemon juice and 30 ml (2 tbsp) water in a dish large enough for the fruit to fit in one layer. Microwave on HIGH for 3 minutes or until bubbling.

3 Arrange the apples in the hot syrup, carefully turning until coated all over. Microwave on HIGH for 5 minutes or until the apples feel cooked when tested with a wooden cocktail stick.

Serve chilled with vanilla ice cream.

COOK'S TIP

To soften ice cream for serving, microwave in the container on MEDIUM for 30–90 seconds, then leave to stand for 1 minute.

Spotted Dick

TIMES		METHOD	SETTINGS	SERVINGS
PREP	**COOK**	MICRO.	HIGH	4
8	10			

75 g (3 oz) self-raising flour

pinch of salt

75 g (3 oz) fresh brown breadcrumbs

75 g (3 oz) shredded suet

50 g (2 oz) soft light brown sugar

175 g (6 oz) currants

about 90 ml (6 tbsp) milk

1 Mix the flour, salt, breadcrumbs, suet, sugar and currants in a large bowl. Add enough milk to give a soft dropping consistency.

2 Spoon into a 900 ml (1½ pint) pudding basin and cover loosely with cling film. Microwave on HIGH for 5 minutes. Leave to stand for 5 minutes. Turn out on to a hot serving plate.

Serve with custard.

Baking

Baked goods, which are light and airy, cook quickly in the microwave. But with baking especially, the microwave has its limitations. Microwaving is a moist form of cooking so it is not possible for baked goods to develop their characteristic brown, crisp surfaces.

Bread
Yeast breads, which depend on a crisp outer crust and soft centre, are best baked in the conventional way though it is possible to microwave bread and finish it off under a hot grill to brown the surface. The microwave can be used to prove bread doughs: microwave the dough on LOW or until doubled in size.

Pastry
The crisp flaky texture of pastry cannot be achieved in the microwave, though suet pastry benefits by the moistness of microwave cooking. Bake pastry in the conventional way and use the microwave to thaw frozen baked pastry and to make pastry fillings.

Biscuits
Flapjacks, cookies and other soft biscuits can be successfully cooked in the microwave. However, they need to be watched carefully due to their high sugar content which causes them to cook in the centre even though the surface may look uncooked. For large batches of cookies, a conventional cooker may be more convenient because it can accommodate more biscuits per batch.

Crisp biscuits are best cooked in the conventional way.

Cakes
Cakes using dark-coloured ingredients such as brown sugar, treacle, dark-coloured spices and chocolate will have greater eye appeal because of their dark colour. Pale-coloured cakes will look more attractive if they are iced or covered with whipped cream.

The choice of container for making cakes is very important. Always use the container size specified in the recipe: if a larger container is used, the cake will cook in less than the given time because a greater surface area is exposed to the microwaves; smaller containers than those specified must not be over-filled. Cake containers must never be more than half full, otherwise the cake, which rises higher in the microwave than it would conventionally, may spill over before it is baked.

Be guided by conventional rules about greasing and lining a cake, but avoid flouring dishes as this produces an unpalatable coating to the cake. Cakes baked in a plastic container will not need greasing and cling flim can be used instead of greaseproof paper, but the cake will have a shiny appearance.

Test cakes by piercing the centre with a wooden cocktail stick; the cake is done if the stick comes out clean. Turn out the cake after it has been left to stand and immediately peel away the paper to prevent it from sticking.

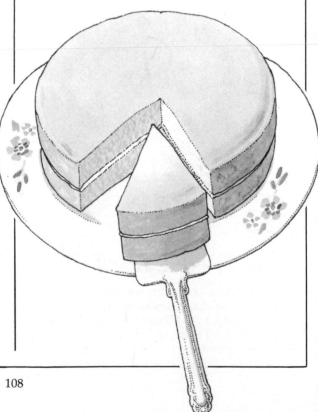

Basic Victoria Sandwich Cake

TIMES PREP 10	COOK 18	METHOD MICRO.	SETTINGS HIGH	SERVINGS 8

175 g (6 oz) self-raising flour

175 g (6 oz) butter or margarine, softened

175 g (6 oz) caster sugar

3 eggs

30–45 ml (2–3 tbsp) milk

jam, to fill

icing sugar, for dusting

1 Grease a 19 cm (7½ inch) deep soufflé dish and base line with greased greaseproof paper.

2 Mix together the flour, butter or margarine, sugar, eggs and 30 ml (2 tbsp) milk in a mixing bowl. Beat until smooth. If necessary, add an extra 15 ml (1 tbsp) milk to give a soft dropping consistency.

3 Spoon the mixture into the prepared dish and microwave on HIGH for 5½–7½ minutes or until a wooden cocktail stick inserted into the centre comes out clean. Give the dish a quarter turn every 2 minutes during cooking.

4 Leave to stand for 10 minutes, then turn out on to a wire rack, remove the paper and leave to cool.

5 When completely cold, split in half and fill with jam. Sieve icing sugar over the top of the cake.

Variations
Orange or **lemon sandwich cake:** replace some of the milk with the finely grated rind and juice of 1 orange or 1 lemon and proceed as above.

Honey Gingerbread

TIMES PREP 10	COOK 12	METHOD MICRO.	SETTINGS HIGH	SERVINGS 8

100 g (4 oz) butter or margarine

150 g (5 oz) clear honey

100 g (4 oz) soft dark brown sugar

150 ml (¼ pint) milk

2 eggs

225 g (8 oz) plain wholemeal flour

5 ml (1 level tsp) ground mixed spice

10 ml (2 level tsp) ground ginger

2.5 ml (½ level tsp) bicarbonate of soda

30 ml (2 level tbsp) crystallised ginger, finely chopped

1 Base line a 11.5 x 23.5 cm (4½ x 9½ inch) ovenproof loaf dish with greaseproof paper.

2 Place the butter or margarine, 125 g (4 oz) honey, half the sugar and the milk in a large bowl and microwave on HIGH for 4 minutes until the butter has melted and the brown sugar has dissolved. Leave to cool.

3 Beat in the eggs, flour, spices, bicarbonate of soda and the remaining brown sugar.

4 Pour into the prepared dish and microwave on HIGH for 7–8 minutes or until a wooden cocktail stick inserted into the centre of the cake comes out clean. Leave to stand until just warm, then turn out on to a wire rack and remove the paper.

5 Place the remaining honey in a small bowl and microwave on HIGH for 20 seconds. Brush over the warm cake and sprinkle with the crystallised ginger.

Chocolate Almond Cake

TIMES PREP	COOK	METHOD	SETTINGS	SERVINGS
15	16	MICRO.	HIGH	8

150 g (5 oz) butter or margarine

100 g (4 oz) caster sugar

2 eggs

45 ml (3 tbsp) clear honey

142 ml (5 fl oz) soured cream

100 g (4 oz) self-raising flour

40 g (1½ oz) cocoa

50 g (2 oz) ground almonds

75 g (3 oz) cooking chocolate drops

15 ml (1 tbsp) brandy

45 ml (3 tbsp) single cream

50 g (2 oz) flaked almonds, toasted

1 Base line a 1.7 litre (3 pint) round casserole with greased greaseproof paper.

2 Cream 100 g (4 oz) butter or margarine and the sugar together until pale and fluffy. Gradually beat in the eggs, honey and soured cream. Fold in the flour, cocoa and ground almonds.

3 Spoon the cake mixture into the prepared tin. Microwave on HIGH for 10 minutes or until a wooden cocktail stick inserted into the centre of the cake comes out clean. Leave to stand for 5 minutes, then cool on a wire rack.

4 Place the chocolate drops, brandy, remaining butter or margarine and cream in a small bowl and microwave on HIGH for 1 minute until melted, stirring once.

5 Pour the icing over the cold cake, allowing it to run down the sides. Sprinkle with the almonds. Leave until set and serve cut into thin slices.

Oaty Apricot Flapjacks

TIMES PREP	COOK	METHOD	SETTINGS	MAKES
15	16	MICRO.	MEDIUM / HIGH	8

175 g (6 oz) dried apricots, finely chopped

30 ml (2 level tbsp) clear honey

100 g (4 oz) butter or margarine

100 g (4 oz) plain flour

100 g (4 oz) soft light brown sugar

pinch of salt

100 g (4 oz) rolled oats

1 Place the apricots in a medium bowl, add the honey and 75 ml (3 fl oz) water and microwave on HIGH for 5 minutes. Cover and leave to stand.

2 Rub the butter or margarine into the flour until the mixture resembles fine breadcrumbs. Stir in the sugar, salt and oats.

3 Press two-thirds of the mixture into the base of a 20.5 cm (8 inch) soufflé dish. Microwave on MEDIUM for 5 minutes.

4 Spoon the apricots evenly over the oats, and sprinkle with the reserved oat mixture. Microwave on HIGH for 6 minutes. Mark into 8 wedges while warm and leave to cool in the dish. When cold turn out and cut into wedges.

COOK'S TIP

If darker flapjacks are preferred, use rolled oats with bran.

Chocolate Fudge Cookies

TIMES PREP.	COOK	METHOD	SETTINGS	MAKES
15	19	MICRO.	MEDIUM	24

100 g (4 oz) butter or margarine, softened

75 g (3 oz) soft light brown sugar

175 g (6 oz) plain flour

30 ml (2 level tbsp) cocoa

1 Grease and line a flat plate or microwave baking sheet.

2 Cream the butter or margarine and sugar until soft and fluffy. Stir in the flour and cocoa to make a smooth dough.

3 Roll the dough into balls about the size of a walnut and arrange 6 in a circle on the plate or baking sheet. Flatten slightly and microwave on MEDIUM for 3½ minutes. Leave to stand for 5 minutes, then cool on a wire rack. Repeat with the remaining dough.

COOK'S TIP

During microwaving, give the plate or microwave baking sheet a quarter turn three times during cooking to produce evenly cooked cookies. This is necessary even in microwave ovens with a turntable.

Chocolate Nut and Raisin Cookies

TIMES PREP.	COOK	METHOD	SETTINGS	MAKES
25	19	MICRO.	MEDIUM	24

100 g (4 oz) butter or margarine, softened

100 g (4 oz) soft light brown sugar

1 egg

30 ml (2 tbsp) milk

100 ml (2 level tsp) baking powder

5 ml (1 tsp) vanilla flavouring

pinch of salt

350 g (12 oz) plain flour

50 g (2 oz) cooking chocolate drops

25 g (1 oz) nuts, finely chopped

50 g (2 oz) raisins

10 ml (2 level tsp) finely grated orange rind

1 Line a flat plate or microwave baking sheet with greased greaseproof paper.

2 Place the butter or margarine, sugar, egg and milk in a large bowl and beat until smooth. Add the baking powder, vanilla flavouring, salt and flour and knead until smooth.

3 Cut the dough in half. Knead the chocolate drops and nuts into one half, and the raisins and orange rind into the other half.

4 Shape the dough into 24 walnut-sized balls, flattening slightly. Arrange about one-third of the pieces in a circle on the plate or baking sheet and microwave on MEDIUM for 3½ minutes. Cool for a few minutes, then carefully remove from the plate and cool on a wire rack. Repeat with the remaining dough.

Sauces

Sauces help to turn simple vegetable and meat dishes into a special occasion as well as to make food go further when necessary. Ice cream or fresh fruits become part of a luxurious dessert when a sweet sauce is poured over them.

With the microwave, sauces become quick and easy to make. Even the more temperamental egg-based sauces such as Hollandaise can be made with less danger of the sauce curdling, and white sauces, based on flour and butter, are less likely to be lumpy. Many sauces can be made in their serving jug or bowl; there is no risk of a sauce sticking to the pan or scorching.

Still, sauces must be stirred frequently. For best results use a balloon whisk for the egg-based sauces and white sauces. Whisking helps prevent the sauce from cooking too quickly and also helps prevent lumps forming. Egg-thickened sauces which are conventionally cooked in a double saucepan such as custard should be gently cooked on LOW in the microwave until the sauce is thick enough to coat the back of a spoon. Remember that these sauces will thicken further during cooling. If a sauce should start to show signs of curdling, quickly open the oven door and start whisking vigorously to arrest cooking.

For sauces which are reduced during cooking to thicken them as with tomato sauces, cook them uncovered until the desired thickness, stirring occasionally with a wooden spoon. Use a large container to help prevent splattering when the sauce bubbles up.

Most sauces can be successfully reheated in the microwave. They can be prepared in advance to free the microwave for preparing other dishes and then reheated. Cover the surface of egg-based sauces and white sauces to prevent a skin forming and store in the refrigerator. Reheat sauces loosely covered. Sauces containing single cream, soured cream, yogurt or eggs all need very gentle reheating on LOW; when possible add these ingredients after reheating the sauce. Vegetables, pasta and meat retain more of their moisture if they are reheated mixed with a sauce.

Frozen sauces can be successfully reheated straight from the freezer. Thaw in the container until the sauce can be removed to a jug or bowl, then reheat, stirring to break up frozen lumps.

Tomato and olive sauce (Sauces) *opposite*

Onion Sauce

TIMES		METHOD	SETTINGS	MAKES
PREP.	COOK	MICRO.	HIGH	300 ml (½ pint)
5	11			

25 g (1 oz) butter or margarine

1 medium onion, skinned and finely chopped

30 ml (2 level tbsp) plain flour

300 ml (½ pint) milk

salt and pepper

1 Place the butter or margarine in a medium bowl and microwave on HIGH for 45 seconds or until melted. Stir in the onion and microwave on HIGH for 5–7 minutes or until soft.

2 Stir in the flour and microwave on HIGH for 30 seconds. Gradually whisk in the milk and microwave on HIGH for 3 minutes, whisking every 30 seconds. Season to taste with salt and pepper.

Serve hot with roast meat, chops, sausages, toad-in-the-hole, vegetable dishes and hard-boiled eggs.

White Sauce

TIMES		METHOD	SETTINGS	MAKES
PREP.	COOK	MICRO.	HIGH	300 ml (½ pint)
3	5			

25 g (1 oz) butter or margarine

45 ml (3 level tbsp) plain flour

300 ml (½ pint) milk or milk and stock mixed

salt and pepper

1 Place the butter or margarine in a small bowl and microwave on HIGH for 45 seconds or until melted.

2 Stir in the flour and microwave on HIGH for 30 seconds or until the surface looks puffy.

3 Gradually whisk in the liquid, using a balloon whisk. Microwave on HIGH for 1 minute, then whisk again to prevent lumps forming.

4 Microwave for a further 1–2 minutes on HIGH until the sauce has thickened, whisking every 30 seconds. Season to taste and serve hot.

Variations

To make a sauce of pouring consistency, use 15 g (½ oz) butter or margarine and 15 g (½ oz) plain flour.

Add the following to the hot sauce with the seasoning:

Cheese sauce: 50 g (2 oz) grated mature Cheddar cheese and a pinch of mustard powder.

Parsley sauce: 30 ml (2 tbsp) chopped fresh parsley.

Hot tartare sauce: 15 ml (1 tbsp) chopped fresh parsley, 10 ml (2 tsp) chopped gherkins, 10 ml (2 tsp) chopped capers and 15 ml (1 tbsp) lemon juice.

Caper sauce: 15 ml (1 tbsp) capers and 5–10 ml (1–2 tbsp) vinegar from the jar of capers.

Blue cheese sauce: 50 g (2 oz) crumbled Stilton or other blue cheese and 10 ml (2 tsp) lemon juice.

Chocolate cherry cups and raspberry jam (Preserves and Confectionary) *opposite*

Tomato and Olive Sauce

TIMES		METHOD	SETTINGS	MAKES
PREP.	COOK	MICRO.	HIGH	450 ml
7	10			(¾ pint)

25 g (1 oz) butter or margarine

1 large onion, skinned and finely chopped

1 celery stick, trimmed and finely chopped

1 garlic clove, skinned and crushed

450 g (1 lb) ripe tomatoes, skinned, seeded and chopped or 397 g (14 oz) can tomatoes

150 ml (¼ pint) chicken stock

15 ml (1 level tbsp) tomato purée

5 ml (1 level tsp) granulated sugar

salt and pepper

50 g (2 oz) stuffed olives, sliced

1 Place the butter or margarine in a large bowl and microwave on HIGH for 45 seconds or until melted. Add the onion, celery and garlic and microwave on HIGH for 5–7 minutes or until the vegetables are soft.

2 Stir in the chopped fresh tomatoes or canned tomatoes with juice, the stock, tomato purée and sugar. Season to taste with salt and pepper. Microwave on HIGH for 10 minutes or until the sauce has thickened, stirring once or twice during the cooking time.

3 Leave to cool slightly, then purée in a blender or food processor. Pour the sauce back into the bowl and add the olives. Reheat on HIGH for 2 minutes and check seasoning.

Serve hot with chops, hamburgers, over vegetables or with pasta.

Variation
Fresh Tomato Sauce: omit the olives and celery. Sieve the sauce after puréeing in step 3.

Bread Sauce

TIMES		METHOD	SETTINGS	MAKES
PREP.	COOK	MICRO.	HIGH	450 ml
5	10			(¾ pint)

6 cloves

1 medium onion, skinned

4 black peppercorns

few blades of mace

450 ml (¾ pint) milk

25 g (1 oz) butter or margarine

100 g (4 oz) fresh breadcrumbs

salt and pepper

30 ml (2 tbsp) single cream (optional)

1 Stick the cloves into the onion and place in a medium bowl together with the peppercorns and mace. Pour in the milk. Microwave on HIGH for 5 minutes, stirring occasionally, until hot.

2 Remove from the oven, cover and leave to infuse for at least 30 minutes.

3 Discard the peppercorns and mace and add the butter or margarine and breadcrumbs. Mix well, cover and microwave on HIGH for 3 minutes or until thickened, whisking after every minute. Remove the onion, season to taste and stir in the cream, if using. Leave to stand for 2 minutes.

Serve hot with roast chicken, turkey and game dishes.

COOK'S TIP

If wished, finely chop the cooked onion and add to the sauce.

Stroganoff Sauce

TIMES		METHOD	SETTINGS	MAKES
PREP	COOK	MICRO.	HIGH	150 ml
10	9			(¹/₄ pint)

25 g (1 oz) butter or margarine

1 medium onion, skinned and finely chopped

125 g (4 oz) button mushrooms, wiped and thinly sliced

5 ml (1 level tsp) French mustard

50 ml (2 fl oz) chicken stock

142 ml (5 fl oz) soured cream

salt and pepper

1 Place the butter or margarine in a medium bowl and microwave on HIGH for 45 seconds or until melted. Stir in the onion and microwave on HIGH for 4 minutes or until the onion begins to soften. Add the sliced mushrooms and microwave on HIGH for a further 2–3 minutes or until the onion and mushrooms are soft.

2 Stir in the mustard, stock and soured cream and microwave on HIGH for 1 minute until hot. Season to taste and serve hot.

This sauce is traditionally served with fillet steak but is equally good with pork escalopes, chicken breasts, gammon steaks or hamburgers.

Hollandaise Sauce

TIMES		METHOD	SETTINGS	MAKES
PREP	COOK	MICRO.	HIGH	150 ml
5	9			(¹/₄ pint)

5 ml (1 tsp) lemon juice

5 ml (1 tsp) white wine vinegar

3 white peppercorns

half a small bay leaf

4 egg yolks

225 g (8 oz) unsalted butter, cut into small pieces

salt and pepper

1 Put the lemon juice, vinegar, 15 ml (1 tbsp) water, peppercorns and bay leaf into a small bowl and microwave on HIGH for 2 minutes or until boiling. Continue to microwave on HIGH for 2–3 minutes longer or until reduced by half. Leave until cold.

2 Strain the liquid into a large bowl. Add the egg yolks and whisk thoroughly.

3 Place the butter in a small bowl and microwave on HIGH for 45 seconds or until melted. Pour into the egg yolk mixture and whisk thoroughly.

4 Microwave on HIGH for 3 minutes whisking every 30 seconds until the consistency of mayonnaise. Season with salt and pepper and serve immediately.

Serve with salmon, broccoli, asparagus and other green vegetables.

Variation
Mousseline Sauce: whip 45 ml (3 tbsp) double cream and stir into the sauce before serving.

Apple Sauce

TIMES		METHOD	SETTINGS	MAKES
PREP	COOK	MICRO.	HIGH	150 ml (¼ pint)
10	7			

450 g (1 lb) cooking apples, peeled, cored and thinly sliced

finely grated rind of 1 lemon

15 ml (1 level tbsp) granulated sugar

15 g (½ oz) butter or margarine

1 Place the apples in a large bowl along with the lemon rind and 30 ml (2 tbsp) cold water. Three-quarters cover with cling film and microwave on HIGH for 5 minutes or until the apples begin to soften. Stir with a wooden spoon and microwave on HIGH for a further 2 minutes or until soft.

2 Add the sugar and butter or margarine and beat to a pulpy consistency. If you wish to make a very smooth consistency, purée in a blender or food processor. Chill in the refrigerator.

Serve cold with roast pork and sausages.

Tuna and Onion Sauce

TIMES		METHOD	SETTINGS	MAKES
PREP	COOK	MICRO.	HIGH	150 ml (¼ pint)
7	10			

25 g (1 oz) butter or margarine

1 large onion, skinned and finely chopped

198 g (7 oz) can tuna fish, drained and flaked

60 ml (4 tbsp) chicken stock

45 ml (3 tbsp) soured cream

2.5 ml (½ level tsp) paprika

salt and pepper

1 Place the butter or margarine in a medium bowl and microwave on HIGH for 45 seconds or until melted. Stir in the onion and microwave on HIGH for 5–7 minutes or until soft.

2 Add the tuna fish, stock and soured cream and stir gently. Microwave on HIGH for 3 minutes until hot. Add the paprika and season to taste.

Serve with tagliatelli and Parmesan cheese, cooked French beans or other freshly cooked vegetables.

COOK'S TIP

To make a homemade stock, microwave chicken bones, seasonings and water for 20 minutes on HIGH, then leave to stand for 20 minutes.

Egg Custard Sauce

TIMES PREP.	TIMES COOK	METHOD	SETTINGS	MAKES
5	8	MICRO.	LOW HIGH	300 ml (½ pint)

300 ml (½ pint) milk

2 eggs

15 ml (1 level tbsp) granulated sugar

few drops of vanilla flavouring

1 Microwave the milk in a large measuring jug on HIGH for 2 minutes or until hot.

2 Lightly whisk the eggs, sugar and vanilla flavouring together in a bowl. Add the heated milk, mix well and strain back into the jug.

3 Microwave on HIGH for 1 minute, then microwave on LOW for 4½ minutes or until the custard thinly coats the back of a spoon. Whisk several times during cooking. The sauce thickens slightly on cooling.

Serve hot or cold with sponge puddings and fruit desserts.

Sweet Whisked Sauce

TIMES PREP.	TIMES COOK	METHOD	SETTINGS	MAKES
10	12	MICRO.	HIGH	600 ml (1 pint)

4 eggs, separated

50 g (2 oz) soft light brown sugar

75 ml (3 fl oz) white vermouth or sweet white wine

1 In a medium bowl, beat the egg yolks and sugar together until pale and creamy.

2 Stir in the vermouth or wine and microwave on HIGH for 2 minutes, whisking occasionally, until the mixture starts to thicken around the edges, then quickly remove from the oven and whisk with a hand-held electric mixer until smooth and thick.

3 Whisk the egg whites until stiff and fold into the sauce. Serve immediately.

Serve with fresh fruit or fruit pies.

COOK'S TIP

This sauce must be served immediately, otherwise the egg white will separate.

Orange Cream Sauce

TIMES		METHOD	SETTINGS	MAKES
PREP	COOK	MICRO.	MEDIUM	450 ml
10	4		HIGH	(¾ pint)

finely grated rind and juice of 3 large oranges

juice of 1 lemon

125 g (4 oz) caster sugar

50 g (2 oz) butter or margarine, cut into small pieces

2 eggs

150 ml (5 fl oz) whipping cream

1 Place the orange rind, orange juice, lemon juice, sugar and butter or margarine in a medium bowl. Whisk in the eggs and microwave on HIGH for 3 minutes, whisking after every minute, then microwave on MEDIUM for 30 seconds or until the sauce has thickened.

2 Remove from the oven and leave to cool. When cold, whisk in the cream.

Serve chilled with plain steamed puddings, ice cream and fruit pies.

Hot Raspberry Sauce

TIMES		METHOD	SETTINGS	MAKES
PREP	COOK	MICRO.	HIGH	150 ml
10	9			(¼ pint)

225 g (8 oz) raspberries, sieved

45 ml (3 level tbsp) redcurrant jelly

15 ml (1 level tbsp) caster sugar

10 ml (2 level tsp) cornflour

5 ml (1 tsp) lemon juice

1 Rub the raspberries through a nylon sieve into a medium bowl. Add the redcurrant jelly and caster sugar. Microwave on HIGH for 2 minutes. Remove from the oven and stir until the jelly has melted and the sugar has dissolved.

2 Blend the cornflour to a paste with 15 ml (1 tbsp) water and stir into the raspberry mixture. Microwave on HIGH for 2 minutes or until thickened, whisking every 30 seconds. Stir in the lemon juice.

Serve hot with steamed puddings or try serving the sauce warm with ice cream and meringue desserts.

Makes 150 ml (¼ pint)

COOK'S TIP

If using frozen raspberries, microwave on LOW for 4 minutes, then leave to stand until completely thawed.

Gooseberry Sauce

TIMES		METHOD	SETTINGS	MAKES
PREP	COOK	MICRO.	HIGH	150 ml (¼ pint)
10	6			

450 g (1 lb) gooseberries, topped and tailed

25 g (1 oz) butter or margarine

45–60 ml (3–4 level tbsp) caster sugar

pinch of ground ginger (optional)

1 Put the gooseberries and 30 ml (2 tbsp) water in a large bowl and three-quarters cover with cling film. Microwave on HIGH for 6 minutes or until the fruit is soft. Add the butter or margarine and caster sugar and stir until the sugar has dissolved.

2 Rub the fruit with juice through a sieve to remove the seeds.

Serve hot or cold with steamed puddings or ice cream.

COOK'S TIP

This sauce is also very good served with mackerel.

Butterscotch Sauce

TIMES		METHOD	SETTINGS	MAKES
PREP	COOK	MICRO.	HIGH	150 ml (¼ pint)
5	5			

170 g (6 oz) can evaporated milk

75 g (3 oz) soft brown sugar

25 g (1 oz) butter or margarine

2.5 ml (½ tsp) vanilla flavouring

15 ml (1 level tbsp) cornflour

25 g (1 oz) raisins (optional)

1 Pour the evaporated milk into a medium bowl and add 30 ml (2 tbsp) water and the brown sugar. Microwave on HIGH for 3 minutes, stirring once. Add the butter or margarine and vanilla flavouring.

2 Blend the cornflour to a paste with a little cold water and add to the bowl, stirring well. Microwave on HIGH for 2 minutes or until thickened, whisking once during the cooking time. Stir in the raisins, if using.

Serve hot with ice cream and puddings.

Preserves and Confectionery

The same conventional principles of making preserves and confectionery apply when making them in the microwave. With preserves and many sweets, sugar is boiled with other ingredients to a desired consistency; during boiling the mixture bubbles up considerably. For this reason, always use a large bowl for making even a small quantity.

Preserves

Choose and prepare fruits and vegetables in the same way as you would when making preserves in the conventional way: fruits for jam need to have sufficient pectin content in order to set; cut the fruit and/or vegetables in a uniform size when making chutneys.

As with traditional jam making, sugar will dissolve more quickly in the cooked fruit if it is first warmed. To do this, microwave the sugar in its bag or in a bowl on HIGH for 3–4 minutes. Stir the sugar into the cooked fruit and it should dissolve in the heat of the fruit. Otherwise, it can be microwaved on HIGH, stirring occasionally, until dissolved.

Fruit and sugar are then microwaved on HIGH for about 15 minutes or until setting point is reached. A conventional thermometer must not be used for testing; use the wrinkle test instead, which is often more reassuring anyway. Spoon a little jam on to a chilled saucer; the jam should wrinkle when pushed with your finger.

Chutneys are cooked for about 30 minutes or until there is no pool of liquid on the surface and the mixture has the consistency of a thick sauce.
Potting: jars can be prepared for potting in the microwave. Fill very clean jars one-quarter full with water and bring to a full boil, remove and pour out the water, then leave the jars to dry upturned on a wire rack. The jars will not all come to the boil at the same time and they should be removed from the microwave using oven gloves. Cover jams and curds with jam pot covers and use vinegar-proof lids for covering chutneys.

Confectionery

Sweet-making need not be a time-consuming and messy task when the microwave is used. Because sugar reaches very high temperatures in the microwave care must be taken. Use oven gloves when handling the bowl and stir the mixture with a long wooden spoon. Do not use a conventional sugar boiling thermometer but test the sugar by dropping a small ball into a glass of cold water to determine which stage the sugar has reached.

Quick sweets can be made by simply melting chocolate and dipping nuts and fruits into it. Chocolate should be microwaved on HIGH just until it looks soft on top. Remove from the oven and stir until melted. Chocolate having a high fat content such as chocolate cake covering and cooking chocolate will melt more quickly than plain dessert chocolate; 100 g (4 oz) cooking chocolate melts in about 3 minutes, dessert chocolate in 4 minutes. Watch chocolate carefully: if left too long in the microwave it will scorch.

Apple Chutney

TIMES		METHOD	SETTINGS	MAKES
PREP.	COOK			900 g
25	30	MICRO.	HIGH	(2 lb)

450 g (1 lb) cooking apples, peeled, cored and finely diced

450 g (1 lb) onions, skinned and finely chopped

100 g (4 oz) sultanas

100 g (4 oz) stoned raisins

150 g (5 oz) demerara sugar

200 ml (7 fl oz) malt vinegar

5 ml (1 level tsp) ground ginger

5 ml (1 level tsp) ground cloves

5 ml (1 level tsp) ground allspice

grated rind and juice of half a lemon

1 Put all the ingredients into a large bowl and microwave on HIGH for 5 minutes or until the sugar dissolves. Stir occasionally.

2 Three-quarters cover the bowl with cling film and microwave on HIGH for 25 minutes, or until the mixture is thick and has no excess liquid. Stir after every 5 minutes during the cooking time to prevent the surface of the chutney from drying out.

2 Leave to stand for 5 minutes and spoon into jars. Cover in the usual way using vinegar-proof tops. Store for 3 months before eating.

Mango Chutney

TIMES		METHOD	SETTINGS	MAKES
PREP.	COOK			450 g
30	25	MICRO.	HIGH	(1 lb)

3 mangoes

2.5 cm (1 inch) piece of fresh root ginger

1 small green chilli, seeded

125 g (4 oz) soft light brown sugar

200 ml (7 fl oz) cider vinegar

2.5 ml (½ level tsp) ground ginger

1 garlic clove, skinned and crushed

1 Peel the mangoes and cut the flesh into small pieces. Finely chop the ginger and chilli.

2 Place all the ingredients in a large bowl and microwave on HIGH for 5 minutes or until the sugar has dissolved. Stir occasionally.

3 Three-quarters cover with cling film and microwave on HIGH for 20 minutes or until thick and well reduced. Stir two or three times during cooking and after every minute for the last 5 minutes to prevent the surface of the chutney from drying out.

4 Stand for 5 minutes and spoon into pre-heated jars. Cover in the usual way. Store for 3 months to mature before eating.

COOK'S TIP

To make a hotter chutney, leave the seeds in the chilli but take care when handling – they can react violently with your skin, causing it to redden and 'burn'.

Raspberry Jam

TIMES		METHOD	SETTINGS	MAKES
PREP	COOK	MICRO.	HIGH	700 g
15	22			(1½ lb)

450 g (1 lb) frozen raspberries

30 ml (2 tbsp) lemon juice

450 g (1 lb) granulated sugar

1 Place the frozen fruit in a large bowl and microwave on HIGH for 4 minutes to thaw. Stir several times with a wooden spoon to ensure even thawing.

2 Add the lemon juice and sugar. Mix well and microwave on HIGH for 5 minutes until the sugar has dissolved. Stir several times during cooking.

3 Microwave on HIGH for 13 minutes, stirring occasionally, until setting point is reached.

4 Pot and cover in the usual way.

Rhubarb and Ginger Jam

TIMES		METHOD	SETTINGS	MAKES
PREP	COOK	MICRO.	HIGH	450 g
15	19			(1 lb)

450 g (1 lb) rhubarb, trimmed weight

450 g (1 lb) granulated sugar

juice of 1 lemon

2.5 cm (1 inch) piece of dried root ginger, bruised and tied in muslin

50 g (2 oz) crystallised ginger, chopped

1 Chop the rhubarb into short even-sized lengths and arrange in a large bowl in alternate layers with the sugar. Pour over the lemon juice. Cover with cling film and leave in a cool place overnight.

2 Remove the cling film and add the root ginger. Microwave on HIGH for 5 minutes to dissolve the sugar, stirring twice.

3 Remove the root ginger, add the crystallised ginger and microwave for 14 minutes or until setting point is reached.

4 Pot and cover in the usual way.

COOK'S TIP

To test for setting point, put a little jam on a chilled saucer and, if set, the surface should wrinkle when pushed with a finger.

Lemon and Grapefruit Curd

TIMES		METHOD	SETTINGS	MAKES
PREP.	COOK	MICRO.	HIGH	900 g (2 lb)
20	7			

grated rind and juice of 2 lemons

grated rind and juice of 1 large grapefruit

4 eggs

225 g (8 oz) caster sugar

125 g (4 oz) unsalted butter, cut into small pieces

1 Place the fruit rind and juice in a large bowl. Using a wooden spoon, beat in the eggs and sugar. Add the butter and stir well.

2 Microwave on HIGH for 7 minutes, or until the curd has thickened. Whisk occasionally during cooking to ensure even thickening.

3 Remove from the oven and whisk for about 5 minutes, or until the curd cools and thickens further. Spoon into pre-heated jars and cover in the usual way.

Lemon and grapefruit curd keeps in the refrigerator for 3–4 weeks.

COOK'S TIP

Lemons and other critrus fruit will yield more juice if microwaved on HIGH for 30 seconds before squeezing.

Coffee and Walnut Fudge

TIMES		METHOD	SETTINGS	MAKES
PREP.	COOK	MICRO.	HIGH	350 g (12 oz)
10	9			

50 g (2 oz) butter or margarine

225 g (8 oz) granulated sugar

90 ml (6 tbsp) milk

45 ml (3 tbsp) coffee essence

50 g (2 oz) walnut pieces

1 Oil a 12.5 × 10 cm (5 × 4 inch) rectangular container.

2 Place the butter or margarine in a large bowl and microwave on HIGH for 45 seconds or until melted. Stir in the sugar, milk and coffee essence and mix well.

3 Microwave on HIGH for 8 minutes or until a drop of the mixture forms a soft ball when dropped in a little cold water.

4 Remove from the microwave oven and beat in the walnuts using a wooden spoon. Continue beating vigorously for about 4–5 minutes until the mixture is very thick, and has become lighter in colour.

5 Pour into the prepared container. Using a sharp knife, mark into squares. Leave to set in the refrigerator overnight. Cut into squares when cold.

COOK'S TIP

Take care when removing sugar mixtures from the microwave oven as they are very hot. Use a tea towel or oven gloves for protection.

Chocolate and Raisin Fudge

TIMES		METHOD	SETTINGS	MAKES
PREP	COOK	MICRO.	HIGH	36
10	3			

100 g (4 oz) plain dessert chocolate

100 g (4 oz) butter or margarine

450 g (1 lb) icing sugar

45 ml (3 tbsp) milk

50 g (2 oz) raisins

1 Place the chocolate, butter or margarine, icing sugar and milk in a bowl. Microwave on HIGH for 3 minutes or until the chocolate has melted.

2 Beat vigorously with a wooden spoon until smooth, then stir in the raisins.

Pour into a 20.5 × 15 cm (8 × 6 inch) rectangular container. Using a sharp knife, mark lightly into squares. Leave in the refrigerator until set. Serve cut into squares.

COOK'S TIP

Only microwave chocolate until it has just melted because it can scorch in the microwave.

Chocolate Cherry Cups

TIMES		METHOD	SETTINGS	MAKES
PREP	COOK	MICRO.	HIGH	12
45	6			

50 g (2 oz) glacé cherries, chopped

30 ml (2 tbsp) kirsch or rum

225 g (8 oz) plain dessert chocolate

1 egg yolk

15 ml (1 level tbsp) icing sugar, sifted

1 Marinate the cherries in the kirsch or rum for at least 1 hour.

2 Meanwhile, make the chocolate shells. Use 24 paper petit four cases to make 12 cases of double thickness, placing them on a baking sheet.

3 Break half of the chocolate into a medium bowl and microwave on HIGH for 3 minutes or until just losing its shape. Stir gently.

4 Spoon a little chocolate into each case and paint it around the edges to coat. Leave to set. Coat again making sure the chocolate forms an even layer. Leave to set in a cool place.

5 Drain the cherries, reserving the kirsch or rum. Peel the paper from the chocolate shells and fill with the cherries.

6 Put the remaining chocolate into a medium bowl and microwave on HIGH for 3 minutes, then add the egg yolk, icing sugar and reserved kirsch or rum. Beat well.

7 Put the mixture into a piping bag fitted with a small star nozzle and pipe into the chocolate shells. Leave to set.

Serve with after dinner coffee and liqueurs.

Index